The Keating Family of Offaly County, I
By Michael T. Tracy

Copyright © 2016 Michael T. Tracy
All rights reserved
ISBN-13: 978-1539856856

Dedication

To the Memories of the Members of the Keating Family

Contents

Dedication

Patrick Keating (1801-1866)

1 Early years	P12
2 Marriage and Family life	P12
3 Pilkington Township, Wellington County	P13
4 Garafraxa Township, Wellington County	P14
5 Death of Patrick Keating	P16
6 Death of Catherine Ann Keating	P18

Patrick Keating (1830-1910)

7 Early years	P21
8 Marriage	P22
9 Death of Patrick Keating	P23
10 Death of Elizabeth Keating	P25

Thomas Keating (1831-1904)

11 Early years	P28
12 Marriage and Family life	P28
13 Death of Thomas Keating	P30
14 Death of Mary Keating	P30

James Keating (1834-1911)

15 Early years	P33
16 Marriage to Mary Daly	P34
17 Death of Mary Keating	P35

18 Marriage to Margaret Cantwell	P35
19 Toronto, Ontario	P38
20 Death of James Keating	P39
21 Death of Margaret Keating	P40

John Keating (1835-)

22 Early years	P42

Arthur Keating (1837-1917)

23 Early years	P43
24 Marriage and Family life	P44
25 Death of Arthur Keating	P49
26 Death of Ann Keating	P51

Mariah (Maria) (Keating) Corbett (1838-1914)

27 Early years	P54
28 Marriage and Family life	P55
29 Chicago, Illinois	P59
30 Will of Maria Corbett	P60
31 A Golden Wedding	P61
32 Death of Maria Corbett	P63

Catherine (Keating) Kirvan (1840-1929)

33 Early years	P65
34 Marriage and Family life	P65
35 Death of Patrick Kirvan	P67
36 Relocation to Toronto and Death	P68

William Keating (1845-1921)

37 Early years	P70
38 Marriage and Family life	P71
39 Death of William Keating	P75

Elizabeth (Keating) Crow (1850-1906)

40 Early years	P78
41 Marriage and Family life	P79
42 Relocation to Toronto	P81
43 Death of Elizabeth Crow	P83
44 Death of Samuel Crow	P83

Thomas Keating (1804-1882)

45 Early years	P85
46 Marriage and Family life	P85
47 Death of Mary Ann Keating	P87
48 Death of Thomas Keating	P88

Thomas Auchmuty Keating (1837-1892)

49 Early years	P90
50 Marriage and Family life	P90
51 Guelph General Hospital	P92
52 Member of the Guelph Board of Education	P92
53 Death of Thomas Keating	P93
54 Death of Eliza Keating	P96

Jemima Mary (Keating) Lamprey (1840-1916)

55 Early years	P98

56 Living with her Brother and His Family — P99

57 Marriage to John Andrew Lamprey — P99

58 Death of John A. Lamprey — P101

59 Death of Jemima Lamprey — P103

Jane Keating (1846-1928)

60 Early years — P106

61 Living with her Brother and His Family — P106

62 Death of Jane Keating — P108

Anna Maria Keating (1848-1930)

63 Early years — P110

64 Living with her Brother and His Family — P111

65 Death of Anna Maria Keating — P112

The Keating Family of Offaly County, Ireland
By Michael T. Tracy

At noon on Easter Monday, 24 April 1916 a hush fell over O'Connell Street in Dublin. From the steps of the General Post Office a man by the name of Patrick Pearse read the Proclamation of the Republic of Ireland: "Irishmen and Irishwomen: In the name of God and of the dead generations from which she receives her old tradition of nationhood, Ireland, through us, summons her children to her flag and strikes for her freedom." Thus began the 1916 Easter Rising to gain independence from England. The Civil War in Ireland had begun. On Friday, 30 June 1922, the Public Records Office of Ireland, located at the historic Four Courts in Dublin, was severely damaged by fire resulting in the loss of a large number of genealogical records of the country. Among these records that were destroyed were the surviving 19th century census returns, two-thirds of the Church of Ireland parish registers and all surviving will probated in Ireland. This destruction was bad enough; however, one has to keep in mind that, Roman Catholic parishes as in the case of the Keating family, simply did not keep accurate records of their parishes dating back to the 17th and 18th centuries. In January of 2001 this author commissioned an extensive search to be conducted by the Offaly Historical and Archaeological Society in the hopes of obtaining further information on the family.

offaly historical & archaeological society

CUMANN STAIRE AGUS SEANDALAIOCHTA UIBH FHAILI

BURY QUAY, TULLAMORE, CO. OFFALY, IRELAND.
Tel. (0506) 21421 Fax: (0506) 21421 email: ohas@iol.ie

Mr Michael Tracy

Your Ref: 703/00

Our Ref:

Date: 08 January 2001

Dear Mr Tracy

Without knowing the Roman Catholic parish your ancestor came from it makes a search quite difficult, however using the dates you supplied us with as a guideline I confirm I conducted a search of the Roman Catholic parish records of all County Offaly (formerly known as King's County) for the marriage record of Patrick Keating to Catherine Ann Walker and I regret to inform you I was unsuccessful in locating the marriage record. I tried every variation of possible name spelling of both Keating and Walker without success. As you can see from our enclosed "Start of Registers" listing, most of the Roman Catholic Marriage registers for the various parishes in County Offaly commence approximately from 1820 to 1830. Civil registration of all Births, Deaths and Marriages only began in Ireland in 1864, therefore for any Marriage or Birth record prior to this date we only have church records to rely on; and if your ancestor's marriage took place in any Roman Catholic parish prior to the commencement of that particular parish registers I'm afraid there will not be any record of the marriage anywhere.

In trying to locate the baptismal record of Thomas Keating for your second request I kept my search open to all of County Offaly but again I was unsuccessful in locating his baptismal record. There was only one record on our files of a Thomas Keating in the same timeframe as your ancestor's birth but unfortunately the parent's names do not match, his details are as follows:

Date	Child	Father	Mother	Parish
5th April 1829	Thomas	Michael Keating	Bridget Jennings	Dunkerrin

Established to promote Offaly History and Heritage

Fig.1. Letter of the Offaly Historical and Archaeological Society, 8 January 2001, Page 1

As I did not have much success in locating either of the two records you requested above I then extended my search and tried to locate a baptismal record for your ancestor Patrick Keating; I was not expecting to be successful as his birth date would have been late 1700's or early 1800's and most of our parish files only commence in the early part of the 19th century. The only baptismal record of a Patrick Keating that fits into the correct timeframe that I could locate was as follows:

Date	Child	Father	Mother	Parish
December 1809	Pat	Martin Keating	A. Corkoran	Eglish

Unfortunately there was no baptismal record of any Catherine Ann Walker in our Roman Catholic Baptismal records for County Offaly that would be consistent with your ancestor's timeframe, it's likely that Catherine's birth may have predated the start of some of our parish registers.

Because we did not have much success in locating the marriage record of Catherine and Patrick Keating or the baptismal record of their first child Thomas I decided to extend my search beyond the confines of the parish records to try to locate any Keating's listed in the Land records. There was one survey conducted in the 1820's called the "Tithe Applotment", this survey is an assessment of Land values for a church tax. Please note not everyone was taxed in this Tithe Applotment as it only taxed *land holders*. I'm enclosing an extract from our index of all Keating's listed in the Tithe Applotment index for County Offaly for the 1820's for your perusal. This survey only lists the name of the person holding land, the name of the Townland where they lived and the Roman Catholic parish they would have belonged to. There are two records of Patrick/Pat Keating in County Offaly, unfortunately we have no way of knowing if either of these Patrick Keating's is your ancestor or related to your ancestor. I'm enclosing two maps of County Offaly detailing how the County is divided up into Roman Catholic parishes and Civil parishes.

It may not be much consolation to you but I have spent a considerable amount of time in dealing with your query and no doubt you will realise I have tried very course open to me at present to come up with the information you require. Very often the query that produces no results take up more time than the positive ones. However should you come up with more specific information in the future (possibly the actual parish your ancestor may have come form) we would be only too glad to have another look at the parish files.

I wish you every success in the future gathering information for your family history.

Yours sincerely,

Helen Flanagan
Research Officer

Fig.2. Letter of the Offaly Historical and Archaeological Society, 8 January 2001, Page 2

To this end the search proved to find no results. Two years later this author personally went to Offaly County. Upon personally researching the surviving Roman Catholic Church records of Eglish Parish and surrounding parishes, this confirmed no outcome of finding older generations of the family which was most unfortunate.

County Offaly was formerly known as Kings County and is located in the Irish Midlands in the province of Leinster. The Keating family history begins with two brothers, Patrick and Thomas. The names of their parents, nor for that matter the exact dates of birth and marriage, presently cannot be determined. However, what is known is that they were born in Eglish Parish and were from a Catholic family.

Patrick Keating (1801-1866): A Tribute to His Life and Times
By His Third Great Grandson, Michael T. Tracy

Patrick Keating was born in Eglish Parish, Kings County now presently called Offaly County, Ireland. Keating would marry while in Ireland and have five children born there before relocating to Canada and settling in Pilkington Township, Wellington County, Ontario. He would farm his lands and would have four more children. This then is the narrative of the life and times of Patrick Keating.

Early years

Patrick Keating was born in about December of 1801 in Eglish Parish, Kings County, Ireland.[1] Due to the lack of record keeping of the Roman Catholic parish of Eglish, baptismal records only begin in January of 1809, thusly a record of Patrick Keating simply does not exist. It is not known who his parents were. Little else is known of Patrick's early years.

Fig.1. Eglish Parish, Offaly County, Ireland, Photograph Courtesy of Michael T. Tracy © 2010 Michael T. Tracy

Marriage and Family life

Patrick Keating met and later married Catherine Ann Walker circa 1830. Little is known of Catherine Ann Walker except that she was born in 1800-01 also in Kings County. The names of her parents are not known. They had five children who were born in Kings County. They were:

Patrick born on Tuesday, 14 September 1830 and died on Tuesday, 20 September 1910;[2]
Thomas born on Wednesday, 20 July 1831 and died on Friday, 19 February 1904;[3]

---

[1] Death Record of Patrick Keating, 28 January 1866, Church of Our Lady Records, Guelph, Ontario, Canada

[2] Death Record of Patrick Keating, 20 September 1910, Ontario, Canada, Deaths, 1869-1938 & Deaths Overseas, 1939-1947. Ancestry.com. Provo, UT, USA: Ancestry.com Operations, Inc., 2010

[3] Death Record of Thomas Keating, 19 February 1904, Ontario, Canada, Deaths, 1869-1938 & Deaths Overseas, 1939-1947. Ancestry.com. Provo, UT, USA: Ancestry.com Operations, Inc., 2010

James born in 1834 and died on Friday, 25 August 1911;[4]
John born in 1835;
Arthur born on Thursday, 15 June 1837 and died on Wednesday, 21 February 1917.[5]

The Keating family left Ireland in 1837-38 and traveled to Canada staying a short time with Patrick's younger brother, Thomas, in Guelph. Thomas migrated to Canada a few years before his brother and by the time his brother arrived in Guelph, Thomas had already established himself there. According to Mr. John Keleher, who wrote an article in the Guelph Historical Society's annual publication, *Historic Guelph*, "Thomas Keating kept the Post Office in the stone store on Lot 1 built for J.D. Oliver next to the hotel which Keating and his brother Patrick occupied on Lot 2."

Pilkington Township, Wellington County

Patrick Keating and his family left Guelph and relocated to Pilkington Township, Wellington County sometime before November of 1838. Patrick was a farmer and raised his family there. Catherine and Patrick had four additional children who were all born in Pilkington Township. They were:

Mariah (Maria) born in November of 1838 and died on Thursday, 13 August 1914;[6]
Catherine born in 1840 and died on Monday, 17 June 1929;[7]
William born on Thursday, 2 October 1845 and died on Wednesday, 19 January 1921;[8]
Elizabeth born on Saturday, 28 September 1850 and died on Thursday, 25 October 1906.[9]

According to the 1851 Canada Census for Pilkington Township, Wellington County, Patrick Keating is listed as being 50 years of age and working as a farmer and his wife Catherine is listed as being 50 years of age with the following children: James age 15; John age 10; Arthur age 7; William age 14; Maria age 11; Elizabeth age 9.[10]

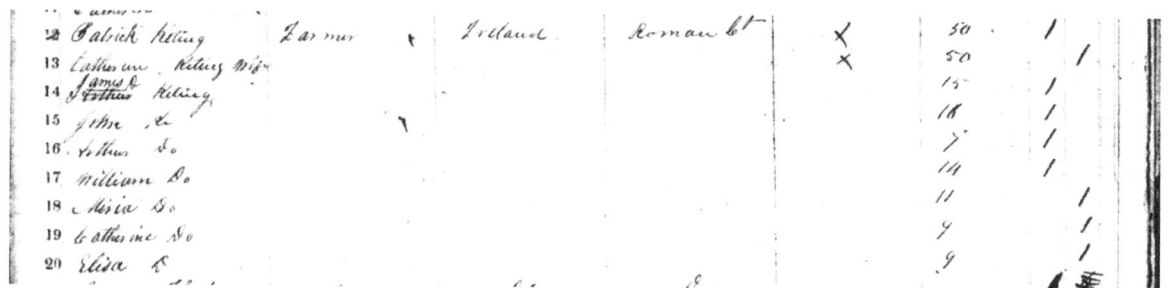

Fig.2. 1851 Canada Census for Pilkington Township, Wellington County, Ontario, Canada listing Patrick Keating and Family

---

[4] Death Record of James Keating, 25 August 1911, Ontario, Canada, Deaths, 1869-1938 & Deaths Overseas, 1939-1947. Ancestry.com. Provo, UT, USA: Ancestry.com Operations, Inc., 2010

[5] Death Record of Arthur Keating, 21 February 1917, Ontario, Canada, Deaths, 1869-1938 & Deaths Overseas, 1939-1947. Ancestry.com. Provo, UT, USA: Ancestry.com Operations, Inc., 2010

[6] Death Record of Maria Corbett, 13 August 1914, Illinois, Cook County Deaths, 1878-1922. Index and Images. Family Search, 2010

[7] Death Record of Catherine Kirvan, 17 June 1929, Ontario, Canada, Deaths, 1869-1938 & Deaths Overseas, 1939-1947. Ancestry.com. Provo, UT, USA: Ancestry.com Operations, Inc., 2010

[8] Death Record of William Keating, 19 January 1921, Ontario, Canada, Deaths, 1869-1938 & Deaths Overseas, 1939-1947. Ancestry.com. Provo, UT, USA: Ancestry.com Operations, Inc., 2010

[9] Death Record of Elizabeth Crow, 25 October 1906, Ontario, Canada, Deaths, 1869-1938 & Deaths Overseas, 1939-1947. Ancestry.com. Provo, UT, USA: Ancestry.com Operations, Inc., 2010

[10] 1851 Canada Census for Pilkington Township, Wellington County, Ontario, Canada; Page 7, Lines 12-20

Garafraxa Township, Wellington County

Sometime before 1863 the Keating family relocated to Garafraxa Township, Wellington County, Ontario, Canada. On Friday, 13 March 1863 Patrick took out a mortgage for $400.00 on his property which was located at the SW ½ of Lot 21, Concession 4.[11]

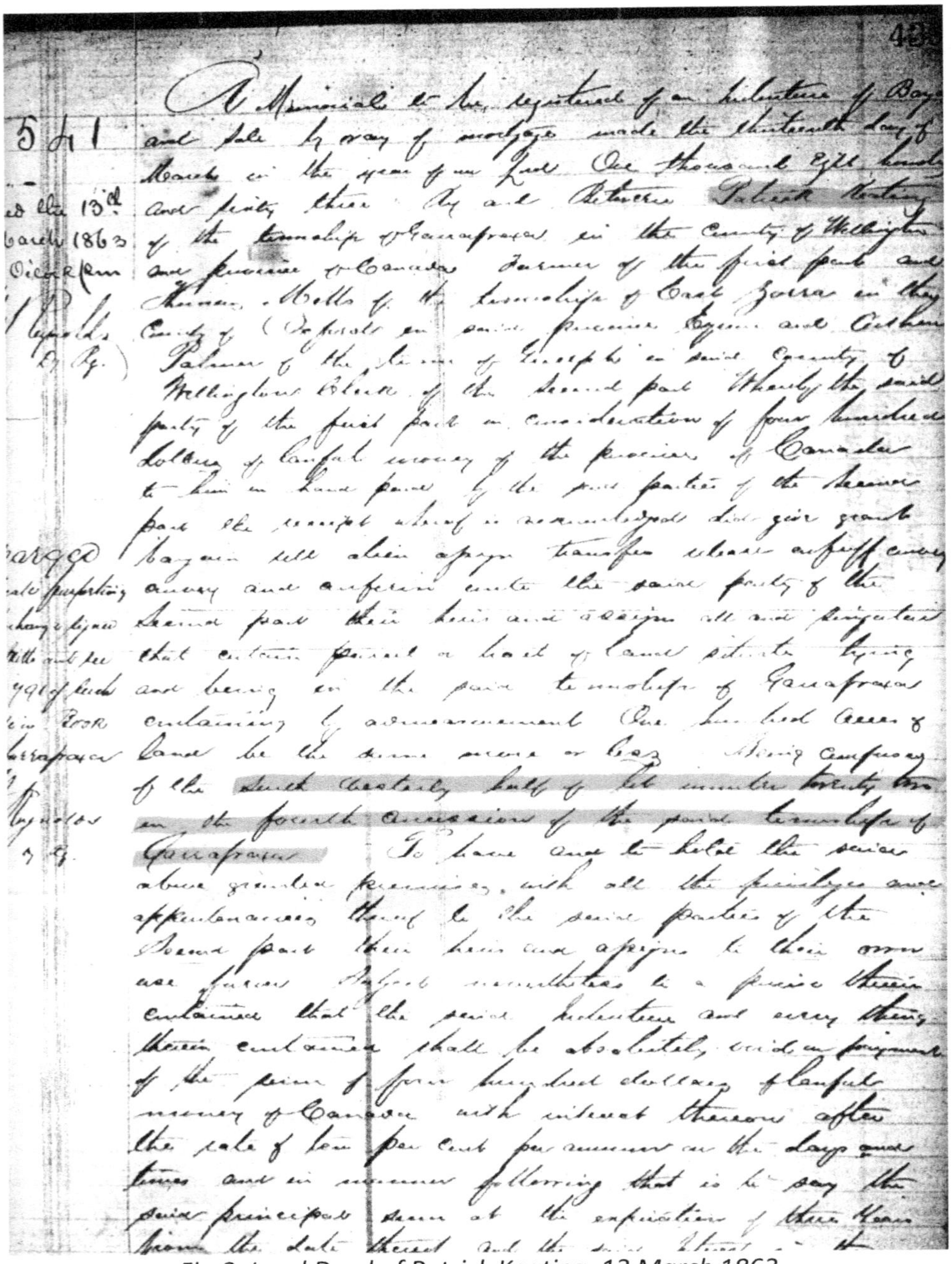

A Memorial to be registered of an Indenture of Bargain and Sale by way of mortgage made the thirteenth day of March in the year of our Lord One thousand Eight hundred and sixty three By and Between Patrick Keating of the township of Garafraxa in the County of Wellington and province of Canada Farmer of the first part and Thomas Mills of the township of East Zorra in the County of Oxford in said province Esquire and Arthur Palmer of the town of Guelph in said County of Wellington Clerk of the second part Whereby the said party of the first part in consideration of four hundred dollars of lawful money of the province of Canada to him in hand paid by the said parties of the second part the receipt whereof is acknowledged doth give grant bargain sell alien assign transfer release and confirm unto the said parties of the second part their heirs and assigns all and singular that certain parcel or tract of land situate lying and being in the said township of Garafraxa containing by admeasurement One hundred acres of land be the same more or less being composed of the South Westerly half of lot number twenty [illegible] in the fourth concession of the said township of Garafraxa To have and to hold the said above granted premises with all the privileges and appurtenances thereto to the said parties of the second part their heirs and assigns to their own use forever Subject nevertheless to a proviso therein contained that the said Indenture and every thing therein contained shall be absolutely void on payment of the sum of four hundred dollars of lawful money of Canada with interest thereon after the rate of ten per cent per annum on the days and times and in manner following that is to say the said principal sum at the expiration of three years from the date thereof and the said interest [illegible]

Fig.3. Land Deed of Patrick Keating, 13 March 1863

[11] Archives of Ontario, Land Deeds, 13 March 1863, Toronto, Ontario, Canada

Fig.4. 1885 West Garafraxa Township Map showing the lands of Patrick Keating and his son, Arthur Keating, Photograph Courtesy of the Wellington County Museum and Archives, Fergus, Ontario, Canada

Fig.5. Farmhouse of Patrick and Catherine Keating and Family, West Garafraxa Township, Wellington County, Photograph Courtesy of Michael T. Tracy © 2010 Michael T. Tracy

Fig.6. Barn of Patrick Keating, West Garafraxa Township, Wellington County, Photograph Courtesy of Michael T. Tracy © 2010 Michael T. Tracy

Patrick Keating is listed in 1866 as residing at Concession 4, Lot 22 in Garafraxa Township.[12]

Death of Patrick Keating

Patrick Keating died on Sunday, 28 January 1866 at his residence in Garafraxa Township of consumption at the age of 64.[13]

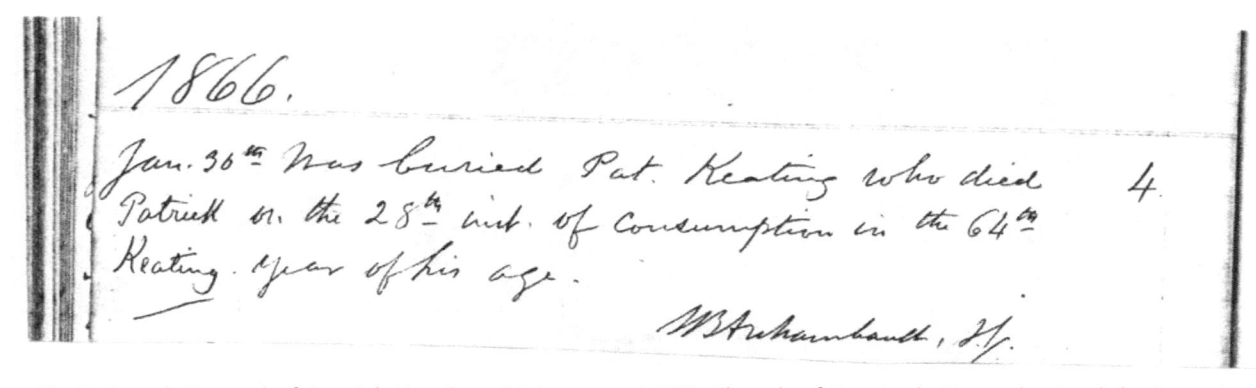

Fig.7. Death Record of Patrick Keating, 28 January 1866, Church of Our Lady Records, Guelph, Ontario, Canada

He was buried in St. Joseph's Catholic Cemetery (Section D-XLIV-9) on Tuesday, 30 January 1866 in Guelph.

---

[12] Rootsweb. Accessed at: freepages.genealogy.rootsweb.ancestry.com
[13] Death Record of Patrick Keating, 28 January 1866, Church of Our Lady Records, Guelph, Ontario, Canada

Fig.8. Grave of Patrick Keating, St. Joseph's Catholic Cemetery, Guelph, Ontario, Canada, Photograph Courtesy of Michael T. Tracy © 2010 Michael T. Tracy

Fig.9. Grave of Patrick Keating, St. Joseph's Catholic Cemetery, Guelph, Ontario, Canada, Photograph Courtesy of Michael T. Tracy © 2010 Michael T. Tracy

Death of Catherine Ann Keating

Catherine Ann Keating died on Saturday, 27 March 1880 of old age in Fergus, Wellington County at the age of 80.[14]

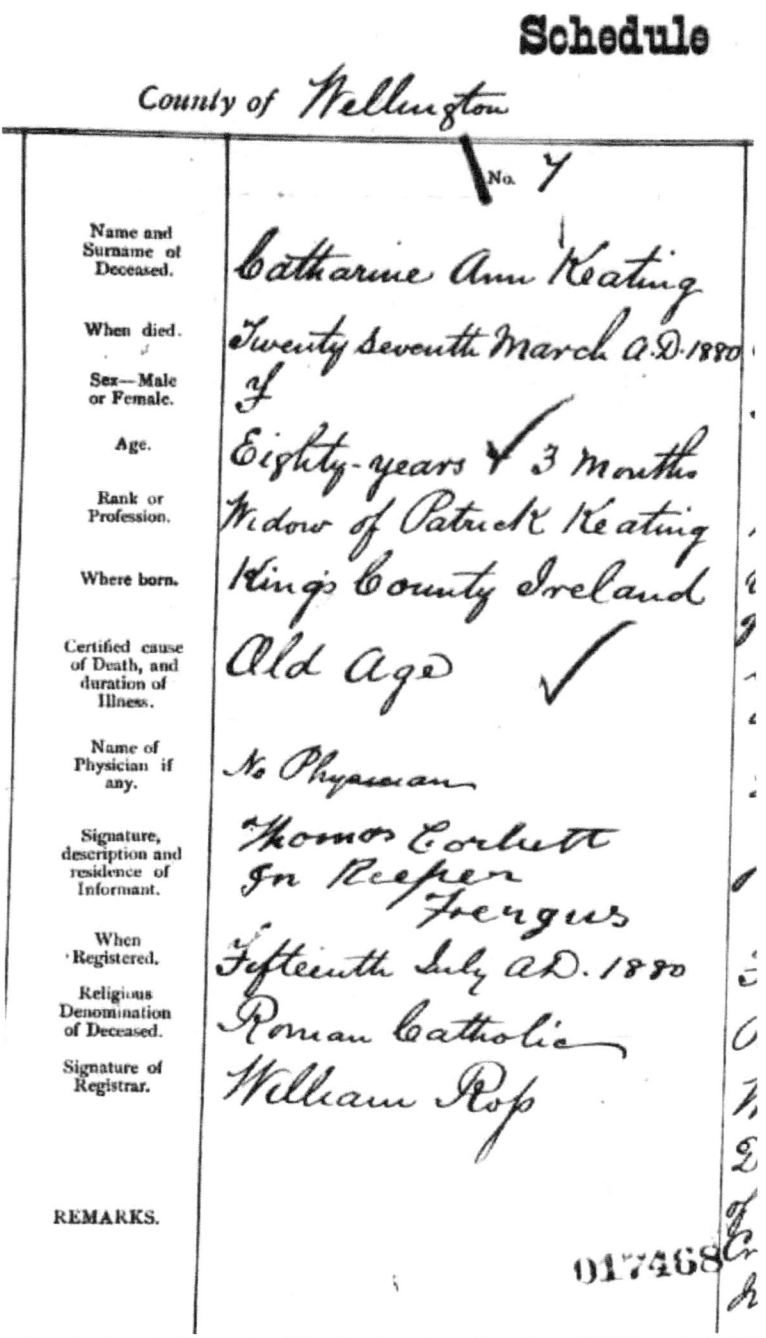

Fig.10. Death Record of Catherine Ann Keating, 27 March 1880

---

[14] Death Record of Catherine Ann Keating, 27 March 1880, Ontario, Canada, Deaths, 1869-1938 & Deaths Overseas, 1939-1947. Ancestry.com. Provo, UT, USA: Ancestry.com Operations, Inc., 2010

She was buried in St. Joseph's Catholic Cemetery (Section A-XI-32) on Monday, 29 March 1880 in Guelph.

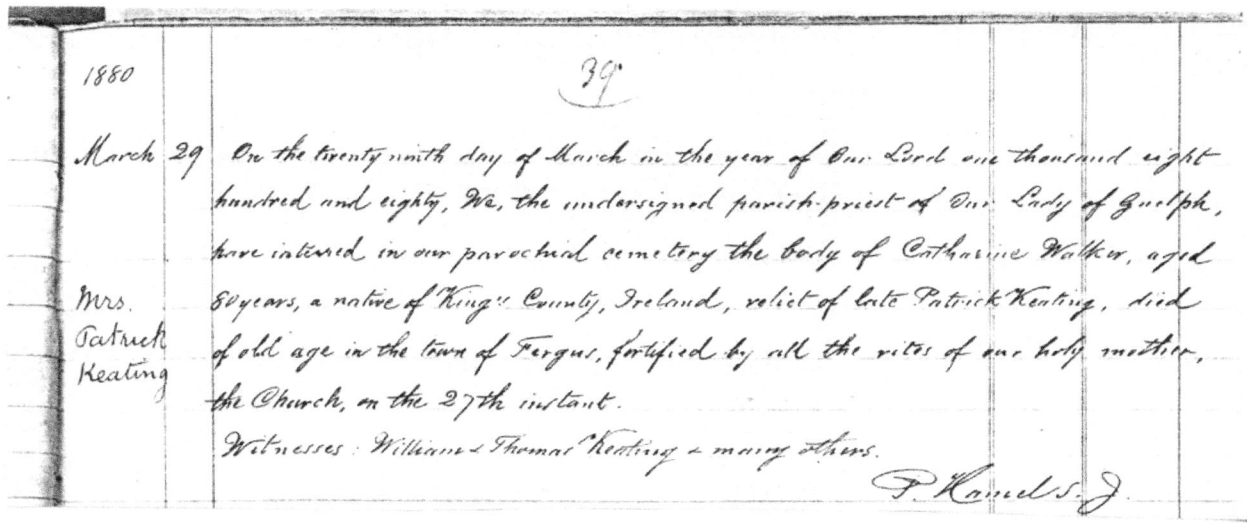

Fig.11. Death Record of Catherine Ann Keating, 27 March 1880, Church of Our Lady Records, Guelph, Ontario, Canada

Fig.12. Grave of Catherine Ann Keating, St. Joseph's Catholic Cemetery, Guelph, Ontario, Canada, Photograph Courtesy of Michael T. Tracy © 2010 Michael T. Tracy

Patrick married Catherine Ann Walker and they would have five children who were born in Ireland. Patrick Keating along with his wife and family left Ireland to pursue a new life in North America. His brother, Thomas was already in Guelph, Ontario, Canada and had been established there. After arriving in Canada the Keating family settled in Pilkington Township, Wellington County, Ontario. There Patrick and Catherine would have four more children. Patrick was a farmer and by 1863 relocated to Garafraxa Township where he lived for the rest of his life.

Patrick Keating is warmly commemorated in grateful esteem and recognition by his third great grandson, Michael T. Tracy. This work is dedicated to the Memory of Patrick Keating.

Memoratus in aeternum (Forever Remembered)

Copyright © 2016 Michael T. Tracy

Patrick Keating (1830-1910): A Tribute to His Life and Times
By His Second Great Grand Nephew, Michael T. Tracy

Patrick Keating was born in Eglish Parish, Kings County, presently called Offaly County, Ireland. As a young boy he traveled with his parents to Canada and settled in Wellington County. He married and had one child, Edward who was born in about 1860 in Wellington County. Keating would, like his father, farm his lands. Having lost his wife, he met and later married Elizabeth O'Kane and the couple settled in Minto Township and later Nichol Township in Wellington County. This then is the narrative of the life and times of Patrick Keating.

Early years

Patrick Keating was born on Tuesday, 14 September 1830 in Eglish Parish, Kings County, presently Offaly County, Ireland.[1] He was the first child of Patrick Keating and Catherine Ann Walker. Very little is known of his early youth. He would travel to Canada with his parents and siblings in 1837-38.

Little is known of Patrick's first wife or when they were married. What is acknowledged is the fact that the couple had a child named Edward who was born in about 1860. Keating is listed as residing in Garafraxa Township, Wellington County at Concession 4, Lot 221 in 1867.[2]

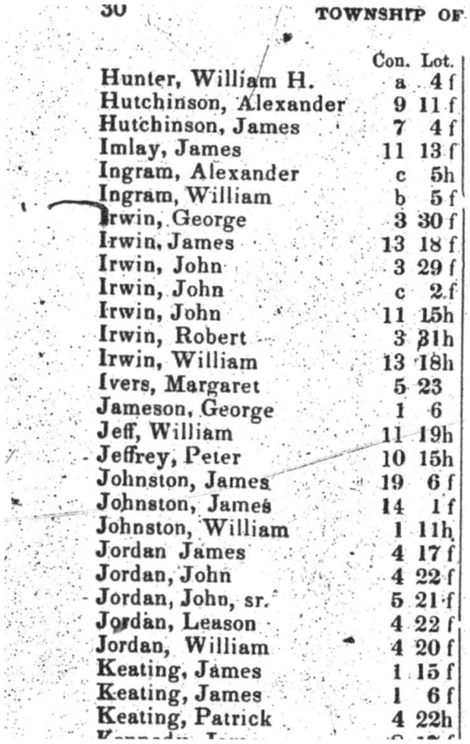
30 TOWNSHIP OF

	Con.	Lot.
Hunter, William H.	a	4 f
Hutchinson, Alexander	9	11 f
Hutchinson, James	7	4 f
Imlay, James	11	13 f
Ingram, Alexander	c	5h
Ingram, William	b	5 f
Irwin, George	3	30 f
Irwin, James	13	18 f
Irwin, John	3	29 f
Irwin, John	c	2 f
Irwin, John	11	15h
Irwin, Robert	3	31h
Irwin, William	13	18h
Ivers, Margaret	5	23
Jameson, George	1	6
Jeff, William	11	19h
Jeffrey, Peter	10	15h
Johnston, James	19	6 f
Johnston, James	14	1 f
Johnston, William	1	11h
Jordan James	4	17 f
Jordan, John	4	22 f
Jordan, John, sr.	5	21 f
Jordan, Leason	4	22 f
Jordan, William	4	20 f
Keating, James	1	15 f
Keating, James	1	6 f
Keating, Patrick	4	22h

Fig.1. 1867 Farmers and Business Directory for the County of Wellington listing Patrick Keating

---

[1] 1901 Canada Census for Elora, Wellington County, Ontario, Canada; Page 4, Line 11

[2] *Farmers and Business Directory for the County of Wellington*, 1867. Canadian City and Area Directories, 1819-1906. Ancestry.com. Provo, UT, USA: Ancestry.com Operations, Inc., 2010

By 1871 his wife is dead and according to the Census for Fergus, Wellington County, Patrick is listed as being 40 years of age, a widow and working as a hostler which is a stableman, and his son Edward is 11 years of age.[3]

Fig.2. 1871 Canada Census for Fergus, Wellington County, Ontario, Canada listing Patrick Keating and Family

Marriage

Patrick Keating met and later married Elizabeth O'Kane. The date of this marriage is also not known. Elizabeth was born on Tuesday, 3 November 1835 in Ireland.[4] By 1881 the couple had relocated to Minto Township in Wellington County and according to the Census it listed Patrick as being 45 [sic] years of age and working as a farmer and his wife Elizabeth is 35 [sic] years of age and Edward is 20 years of age and also working as a farmer.[5]

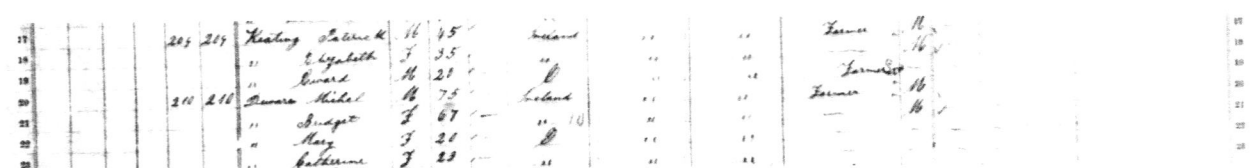

Fig.3. 1881 Canada Census for Minto Township, Wellington County, Ontario, Canada listing Patrick Keating and Family

By 1891 the Keatings are residing in Minto Township with Patrick being 60 [sic] years of age and working as a farmer and his wife Elizabeth is listed as being 45 [sic] years of age.[6]

Fig.4. 1891 Canada Census for Minto Township, Wellington County, Ontario, Canada listing Patrick and Elizabeth Keating

---

[3] 1871 Canada Census for Fergus, Wellington County, Ontario, Canada; Page 30, Lines 19-20

[4] 1901 Canada Census for Elora, Wellington County, Ontario, Canada; Page 4, Line 12

[5] 1881 Canada Census for Minto Township, Wellington County, Ontario, Canada; Page 52, Lines 17-19

[6] 1891 Canada Census for Minto Township, Wellington County, Ontario, Canada; Page 36, Lines 9-10

According to the 1901 Canada Census for Elora, Wellington County, Patrick is listed as being 70 years of age and working as a farmer and his wife Elizabeth is 65 years of age.[7]

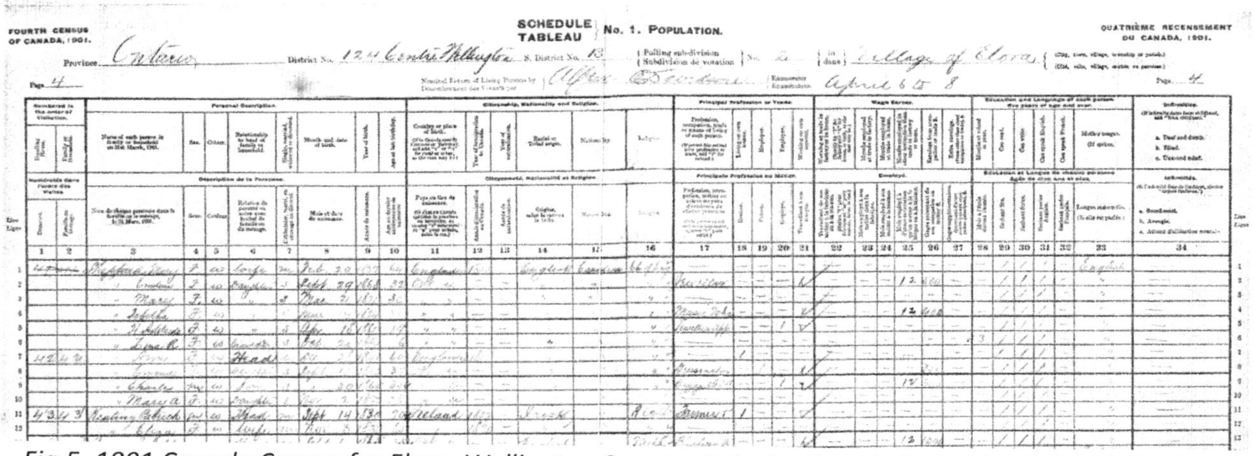
FOURTH CENSUS OF CANADA, 1901.

SCHEDULE No. 1. POPULATION.
TABLEAU

QUATRIÈME RECENSEMENT DU CANADA, 1901.

Province Ontario — District No. 124 Centre Wellington — S. District No. 13 — Village of Elora

Page 4

Fig.5. 1901 Canada Census for Elora, Wellington County, Ontario, Canada listing Patrick and Elizabeth Keating

Death of Patrick Keating

Patrick Keating died on Tuesday, 20 September 1910 at Salem, Nichol Township, Wellington County of senile debility at the age of 80.[8]

---

7 1901 Canada Census for Elora, Wellington County, Ontario, Canada; Page 4, Lines 11-12

8 Death Record of Patrick Keating, 20 September 1910, Ontario, Canada, Deaths, 1869-1938 & Deaths Overseas, 1939-1947. Ancestry.com. Provo, UT, USA: Ancestry.com Operations, Inc., 2010

Division of (1) Nichol

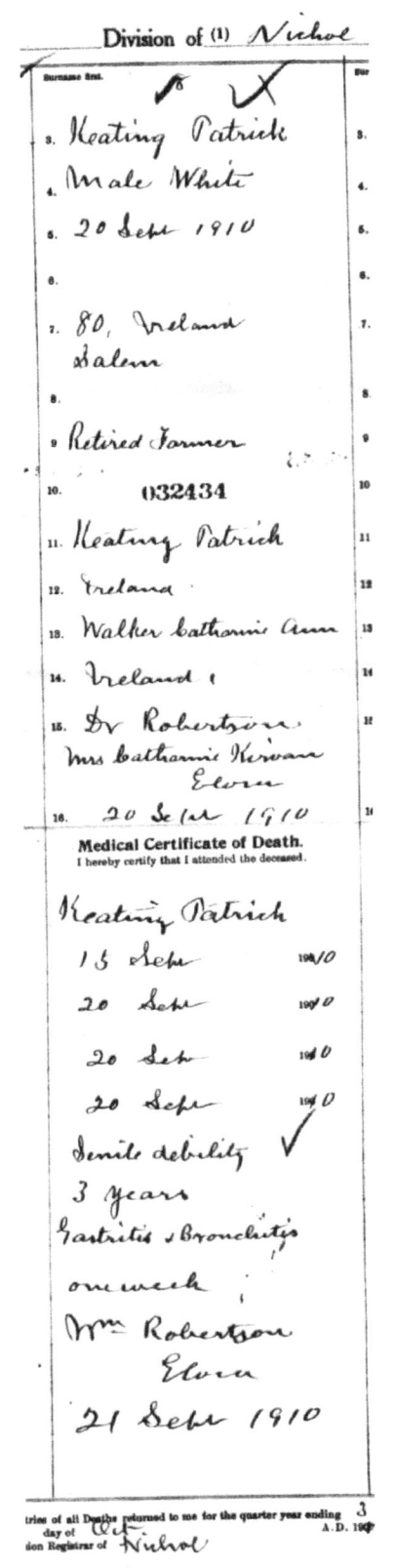

3. Keating Patrick
4. Male White
5. 20 Sept 1910
6.
7. 80, Ireland
   Salem
8.
9. Retired Farmer
10. 032434
11. Keating Patrick
12. Ireland
13. Walker Catharine Ann
14. Ireland
15. Dr Robertson
    Mrs Catharine Kirwan
    Elora
16. 20 Sept 1910

Medical Certificate of Death.
I hereby certify that I attended the deceased.

Keating Patrick
13 Sept   1910
20 Sept   1910
20 Sept   1910
20 Sept   1910
Senile debility ✓
3 years
Gastritis & Bronchitis
one week
Wm Robertson
Elora
21 Sept 1910

tries of all Deaths returned to me for the quarter year ending 3 day of Oct A.D. 1910
ion Registrar of Nichol

Fig.6. Death Record of Patrick Keating, 20 September 1910

He was buried on Thursday, 22 September 1910 at St. Mary Immaculate Cemetery (Section C-2-1) in Elora.

Death of Elizabeth Keating

Elizabeth Keating died on Friday, 12 November 1915 at Guelph of old age at the age of 80.[9]

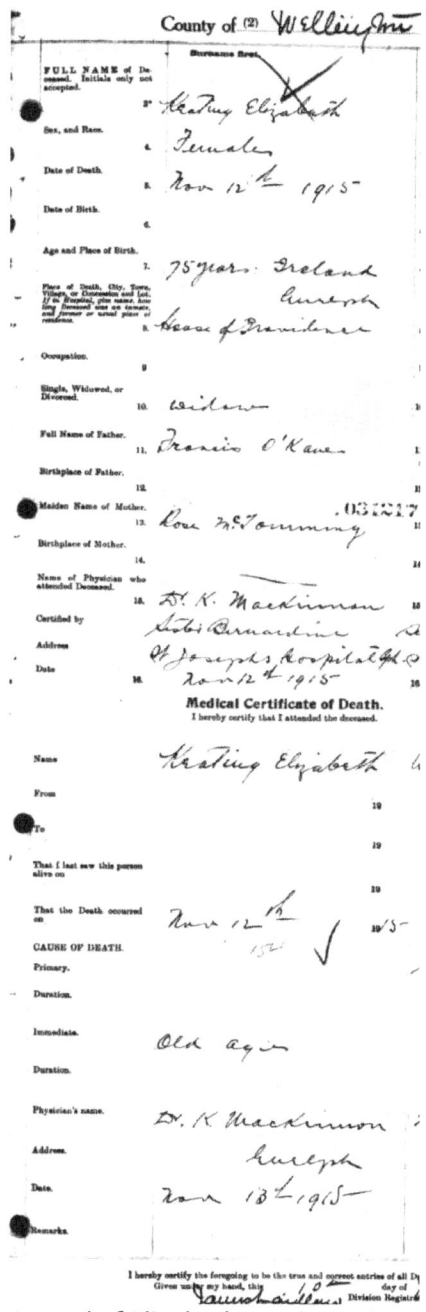

Fig.7. Death Record of Elizabeth Keating, 12 November 1915

---

[9] Death Record of Elizabeth Keating, 12 November 1915, Ontario, Canada, Deaths, 1869-1938 & Deaths Overseas, 1939-1947. Ancestry.com. Provo, UT, USA: Ancestry.com Operations, Inc., 2010

She was buried next to her husband on Sunday, 14 November 1915 at St. Mary Immaculate Cemetery (Section C-2-1) in Elora.

Fig.8. Graves of Patrick and Elizabeth Keating, St. Mary Immaculate Cemetery, Elora, Photograph Courtesy of Michael T. Tracy © 2010 Michael T. Tracy

Patrick Keating is warmly commemorated in grateful esteem and recognition by his second great grand-nephew, Michael T. Tracy. This work is dedicated to the Memory of Patrick Keating.

Memoratus in aeternum (Forever Remembered)

Copyright © 2016 Michael T. Tracy

Thomas Keating (1831-1904): A Tribute to His Life and Times
By His Second Great Grand Nephew, Michael T. Tracy

As a young boy, Thomas Keating traveled with his parents and siblings to Canada from Eglish Parish, Kings County, presently, Offaly County, Ireland in 1837-38. The family settled in Wellington County, Ontario. Thomas would marry and have nine children who were all born in Pilkington Township, Wellington County. Like his father he was a life-long farmer. This then is the narrative of the life and times of Thomas Keating.

Early years

Thomas Keating was born on Wednesday, 20 July 1831 in Eglish Parish, Kings County, presently, Offaly County, Ireland.[1] He was the second child of Patrick Keating and Catherine Ann Walker. Very little is known of his early youth. He would travel to Canada with his parents and siblings in 1837-38 to a new world away from Ireland. By 1861 Thomas is residing in Pilkington Township, Wellington County and is listed as being 33 years of age and working as a laborer.[2]

Marriage and Family life

Thomas Keating met and later married Mary Duggan on Thursday, 4 February 1864 in Pilkington Township by the Reverend John B. Archambault. The witnesses to the marriage were James Purvis and Thomas's sister Elizabeth Keating. The couple had nine children who were all born in Pilkington Township. They were:

Margaret Teresa born on Sunday, 23 September 1866[3] and died in 1951;
Catherine Ann born in February of 1867[4] and died on Tuesday, 23 September 1924;[5]
John born on Monday, 23 December 1867[6] and died on Tuesday, 28 December 1937;[7]
Mary (Ellen) born on Thursday, 4 November 1869[8] and died in 1947;
Arthur Joseph born on December of 1872[9] and died on Wednesday, 24 June 1931;[10]
Christina (Justina) born on Saturday, 25 May 1878[11] and died on Wednesday, 10 October 1945;
Thomas James born on Friday, 27 August 1880;
Mary Bertha born on Saturday, 12 August 1882 and died in December of 1964;
William Francis born on Thursday, 9 April 1885[12] and died on Sunday, 11 June 1899.[13]

---

[1] 1901 Canada Census for Pilkington Township, Wellington County, Ontario, Canada; Page 4, Line 47
[2] 1861 Canada Census for Pilkington Township, Wellington County, Ontario, Canada; Page 30, Line 13
[3] Baptismal Record of Margaret Teresa Keating, 23 September 1866, Church of Our Lady Records, Guelph, Ontario, Canada
[4] Baptismal Record of Catherine Ann Keating, 6 March 1867, Church of Our Lady Records, Guelph, Ontario, Canada
[5] Death Record of Catherine A. McDonald, 23 September 1924, Ontario, Canada, Deaths 1869-1938 & Deaths Overseas, 1939-1947. Ancestry.com. Provo, UT, USA: Ancestry.com Operations, Inc., 2010
[6] Baptismal Record of John Keating, 1 January 1868, Church of Our Lady Records, Guelph, Ontario, Canada
[7] Death Record of John Keating, 28 December 1937, Ontario, Canada, Deaths 1869-1938 & Deaths Overseas, 1939-1947. Ancestry.com. Provo, UT, USA: Ancestry.com Operations, Inc., 2010
[8] Baptismal Record of Mary (Ellen) Keating, 16 December 1869, Church of Our Lady Records, Guelph, Ontario, Canada
[9] Baptismal Record of Arthur Joseph Keating, 3 March 1872, Church of Our Lady Records, Guelph, Ontario, Canada
[10] Death Record of Arthur J. Keating, 24 June 1931, Ontario, Canada, Deaths 1869-1938 & Deaths Overseas, 1939-1947. Ancestry.com. Provo, UT, USA: Ancestry.com Operations, Inc., 2010
[11] Baptismal Record of Christina (Justina) Keating, 30 May 1878, Church of Our Lady Records, Guelph, Ontario, Canada
[12] Baptismal Record of William Francis Keating, 30 April 1885, Church of Our Lady Records, Guelph, Ontario, Canada

Thomas Keating and his family resided on Concession 2, Lot 13 in Pilkington Township, Wellington County beginning in 1867.[14]

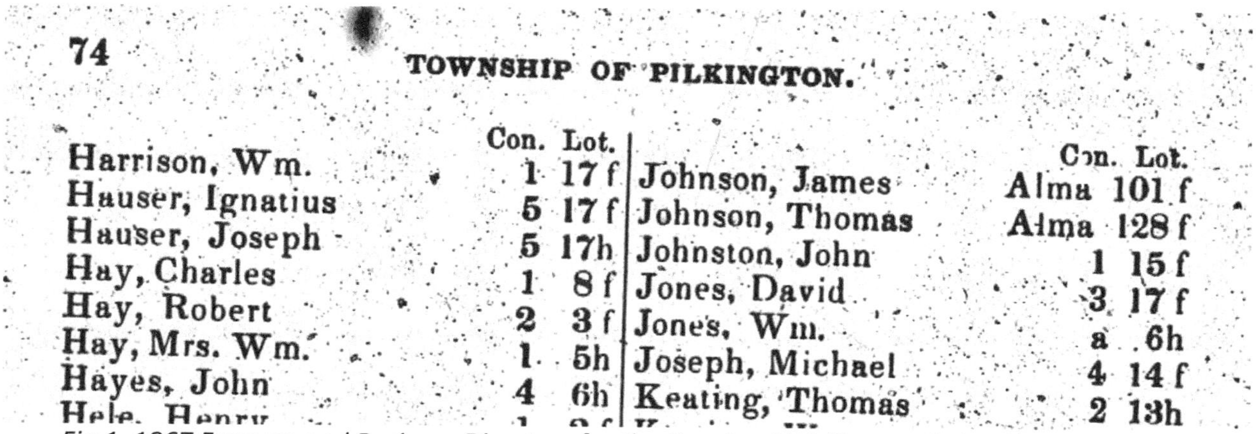

74 TOWNSHIP OF PILKINGTON.

	Con.	Lot.		Con.	Lot.
Harrison, Wm.	1	17 f	Johnson, James	Alma	101 f
Hauser, Ignatius	5	17 f	Johnson, Thomas	Alma	128 f
Hauser, Joseph	5	17h	Johnston, John	1	15 f
Hay, Charles	1	8 f	Jones, David	3	17 f
Hay, Robert	2	3 f	Jones, Wm.	a	6h
Hay, Mrs. Wm.	1	5h	Joseph, Michael	4	14 f
Hayes, John	4	6h	Keating, Thomas	2	13h

Fig.1. 1867 Farmers and Business Directory for the County of Wellington listing Thomas Keating

According to the 1871 Canada Census for Pilkington Township, Wellington County, Thomas is listed as being 40 years of age and working as a farmer and his wife Mary is listed as being 29 years of age with the following children: Catherine age 6; Margaret age 4; John age 3 and Mary Ellen age 1.[15]

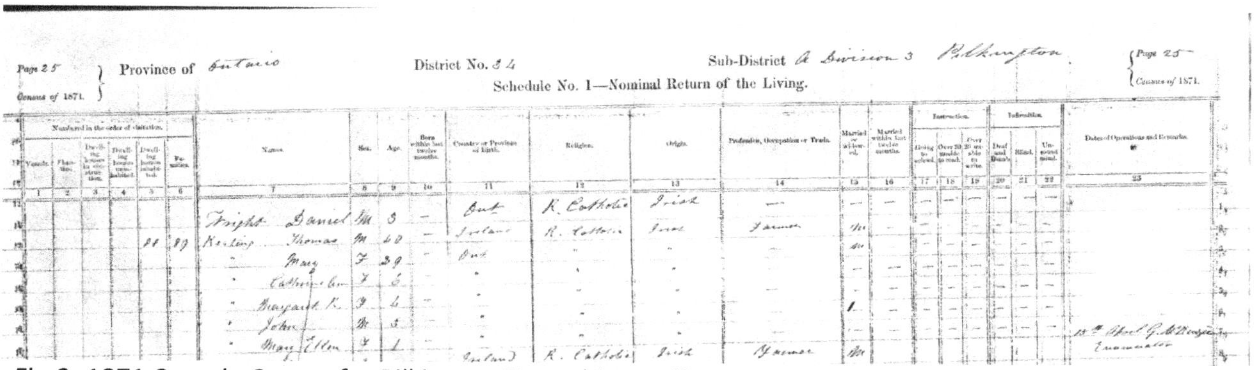

Page 25 Census of 1871. Province of Ontario District No. 34 Sub-District A Division 3 Pilkington
Schedule No. 1—Nominal Return of the Living.

Names	Sex	Age	Country or Province of Birth	Religion	Origin	Profession, Occupation or Trade	Married or widowed
Wright Daniel	M	3	Ont	R. Catholic	Irish		
Keating Thomas	M	40	Ireland	R. Catholic	Irish	Farmer	M
Mary	F	29	Ont				M
Catherine	F	6					
Margaret	F	4					
John	M	3					
Mary Ellen	F	1					

Fig.2. 1871 Canada Census for Pilkington Township, Wellington County, Ontario, Canada listing Thomas Keating and Family

The Keating family by 1881 is listed in the 1881 Canada Census for Pilkington Township showing Thomas as being 45 years of age and working as a farmer and his wife Mary is 39 years of age with the following children: Catherine age 14; Margaret age 13; John age 12; Mary age 10; Arthur age 8; Christina age 5 and Thomas age 3.[16]

---

[13] Death Record of William F. Keating, 11 June 1899, Ontario, Canada, Deaths 1869-1938 & Deaths Overseas, 1939-1947. Ancestry.com. Provo, UT, USA: Ancestry.com Operations, Inc., 2010

[14] *Farmers and Business Directory for the County of Wellington*, 1867-1884. Canadian City and Area Directories, 1819-1906. Ancestry.com. Provo, UT, USA: Ancestry.com Operations, Inc., 2010

[15] 1871 Canada Census for Pilkington Township, Wellington County, Ontario, Canada; Page 25, Lines 12-17

[16] 1881 Canada Census for Pilkington Township, Wellington County, Ontario, Canada; Pages 18-19, Lines 25-8

By 1891 the Keatings have relocated to Nichol Township, Wellington County, with the Census listing Thomas as being 50 [sic] years of age and working as a farmer and Mary is also 50 [sic] years of age with the following children: Arthur age 18 and working as a farmer; Christina age 14; Mary age 8 and William age 6.[17]

According to the 1901 Canada Census the family has relocated back to Pilkington Township with Thomas Keating listed as being 68 years of age and working as a farmer and his wife Mary is 60 years of age with the following children: Joseph age 27 and working as a farmer; Thomas age 20 and working as a farmer and Bertha age 15.[18]

Death of Thomas Keating

Thomas Keating died on Friday, 19 February 1904 of heart disease at the age of 72 in Nichol Township, Wellington County.[19]

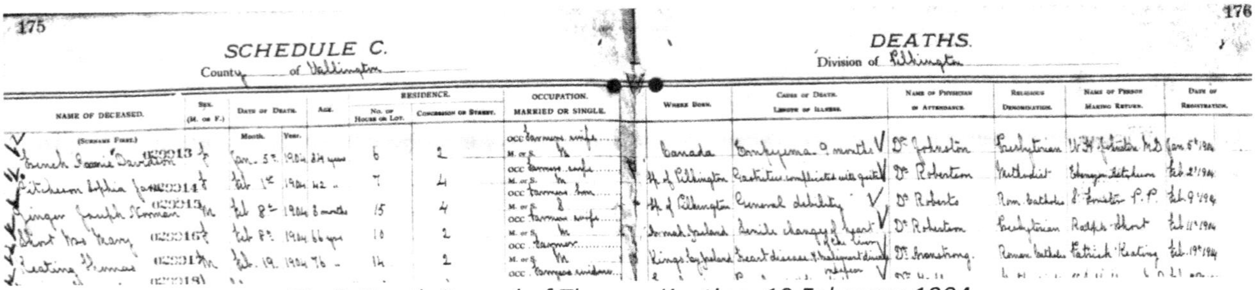

Fig.3. Death Record of Thomas Keating, 19 February 1904

He was buried in St. Joseph's Roman Catholic Cemetery (Section D-37) in Guelph on Sunday, 21 February 1904.

Death of Mary Keating

After her husband's death Mary Keating moved to Guelph where she resided for a short period of time.[20] Mary Keating died on Friday, 25 December 1925 at the age of 85 in Pilkington Township.[21]

---

[17] 1891 Canada Census for Nichol Township, Wellington County, Ontario, Canada; Pages 11-12, Lines 22-2

[18] 1901 Canada Census for Pilkington Township, Wellington County, Ontario, Canada; Page 4-5, Lines 47-2

[19] Death Record of Thomas Keating, 19 February 1904, Ontario, Canada, Deaths 1869-1938 & Deaths Overseas, 1939-1947. Ancestry.com. Provo, UT, USA: Ancestry.com Operations, Inc., 2010

[20] 1911 Canada Census for Guelph, Wellington County, Ontario, Canada; Page 8, Line 9

[21] Death Record of Mary Keating, 25 December 1925, Ontario, Canada, Deaths 1869-1938 & Deaths Overseas, 1939-1947. Ancestry.com. Provo, UT, USA: Ancestry.com Operations, Inc., 2010

471

Shington

No. 8 034678

Keating
Mary
Con 2, 3 Lot 14

Female | Irish | Widowed
82 yrs

H of Nichol | 1848
Retired farm wife
farming

from 1920 to Dec 25 1925

Timothy Duggan
Ireland
Elizabeth McGinn
Ireland
H. O. Howitt
Guelph Ont
Thomas Keating
R.R. Ariss Ont
Son
R.C. Cemetery - Guelph
Dec 28 1925
J. A. McDermott
Guelph Ont
Senile Arterial Changes
Dec 25 1925

MEDICAL CERTIFICATE OF DEATH

Mary Keating
Dec 25 1925

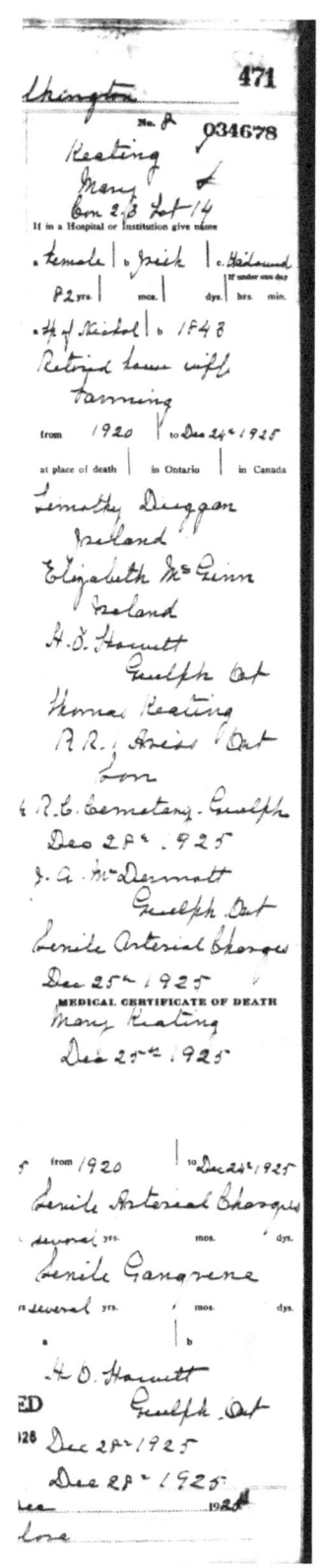

from 1920 to Dec 25 1925
Senile Arterial Changes
several yrs

Senile Gangrene
several yrs

H. O. Howitt
Guelph Ont
Dec 28 1925
Dec 28 1925

Fig. 4. Death Record of Mary Keating, 25 December 1925

She was buried next to her husband on Monday, 28 December 1925 in St. Joseph's Roman Catholic Cemetery (Section D-37) in Guelph.

Thomas Keating is warmly commemorated in grateful esteem and recognition by his second great grand-nephew, Michael T. Tracy. This work is dedicated to the Memory of Thomas Keating.

Memoratus in aeternum (Forever Remembered)

Copyright © 2016 Michael T. Tracy

James Keating (1834-1911): A Tribute to His Life and Times
By His Second Great Grand Nephew, Michael T. Tracy

James Keating was born in Eglish Parish, Kings County, presently, Offaly County, Ireland. He traveled with his parents and siblings to Canada settling in Pilkington Township, Wellington County, Ontario. James was a farmer, married twice and had 14 children. This then is the narrative of the life and times of James Keating.

Early years

James Keating was born in 1834 in Eglish Parish, Kings County, presently, Offaly County, Ireland. He was the third child of Patrick Keating and Catherine Ann Walker. Very little is known of his early youth. He traveled to Canada with his family in 1837-38. He is listed in the 1851 Canada Census for Pilkington Township, Wellington County, Ontario, Canada as being 15 years of age.[1]

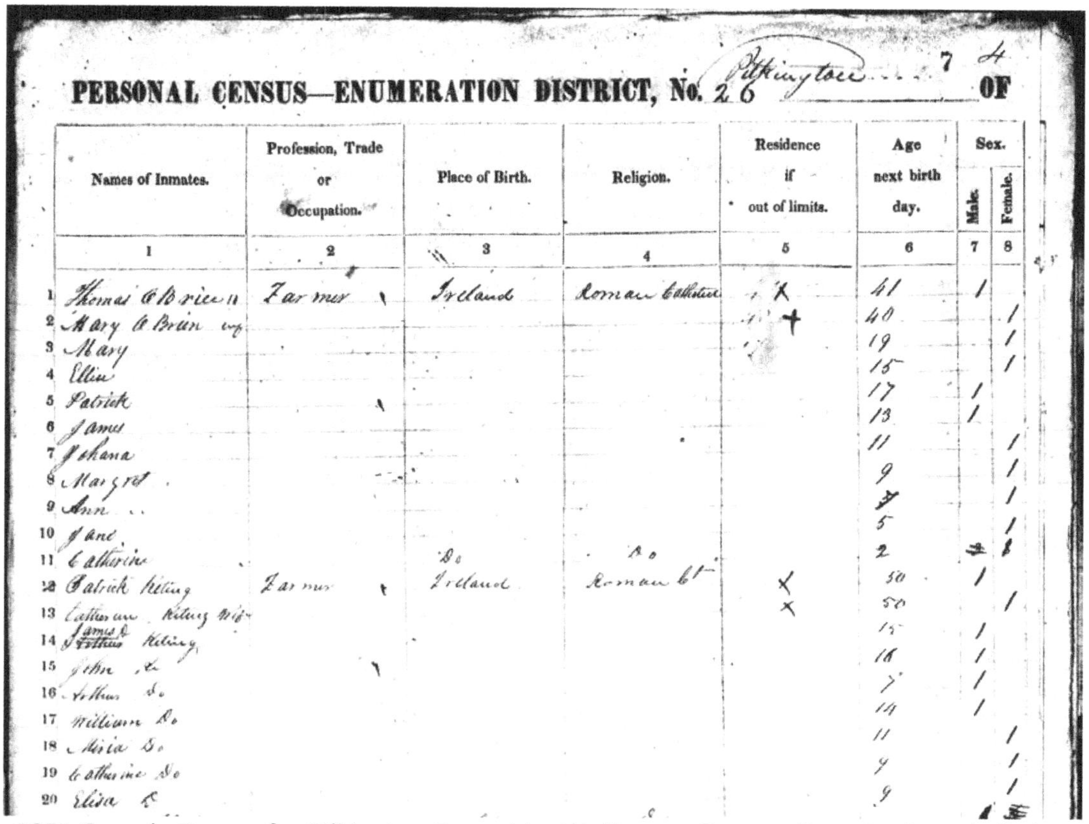
PERSONAL CENSUS—ENUMERATION DISTRICT, No. 26 Pilkington 7 OF

	Names of Inmates.	Profession, Trade or Occupation.	Place of Birth.	Religion.	Residence if out of limits.	Age next birth day.	Male.	Female.
	1	2	3	4	5	6	7	8
1	Thomas O'Brien	Farmer	Ireland	Roman Catholic	X	41	1	
2	Mary O'Brien wife				+	40		1
3	Mary					19		1
4	Ellen					15		1
5	Patrick					17	1	
6	James					13	1	
7	Johana					11		1
8	Margret					9		1
9	Ann					7		1
10	Jane					5		1
11	Catherine		Do	Do		2		1
12	Patrick Keting	Farmer	Ireland	Roman Ct	X	50	1	
13	Catherine Keting wife				X	50		1
14	James Keting					15	1	
15	John Do					16	1	
16	Arthur Do					7	1	
17	William Do					14	1	
18	Maria Do					11		1
19	Catherine Do					9		1
20	Eliza Do					9		1

Fig.1. 1851 Canada Census for Pilkington Township, Wellington County, Ontario, Canada listing James Keating (Line 14)

[1] 1851 Canada Census for Pilkington Township, Wellington County, Ontario, Canada; Page 7, Line 14

Marriage to Mary Daly

James Keating met and later married Mary Daly in 1852-53. Mary was born in about 1835 in Nichol Township, Wellington County. The couple resided in Garafraxa Township, Wellington County where all of their nine children were born. They were:

Arthur Thomas born on Friday, 17 March 1854[2] and died on Saturday, 17 June 1922;[3]
John Patrick born on Friday, 17 March 1854[4] and died on Monday, 1 October 1928;[5]
Ann Teresa born in December of 1856 and died on Wednesday, 9 January 1929;[6]
Catherine born on Thursday, 1 November 1860;[7]
Peter James born in September of 1862 and died in 1939;
William born in 1864 and died on Monday, 18 February 1924;[8]
Mary Ellen born in 1868;
Margaret born on Saturday, 15 October 1870[9]
Ellen Maria born on Saturday, 2 September 1871;[10]

The Keating family is listed in the 1871 Canada Census for West Garafraxa Township, Wellington County with James being 37 years of age and working as a farmer and his wife Mary is listed as being 36 years of age with the following children: John age 17 and working as a farmer; Arthur age 17 and working as a farmer; Ann age 15; Catherine age 11; Peter age 9; William age 7; Mary Ellen age 3 and Ellen Maria age 1.[11]

---

[2] 1901 Canada Census for Nichol Township, Wellington County, Ontario, Canada; Page 1, Line 41

[3] Death Record of Arthur T. Keating, 17 June 1922, Ontario, Canada, Deaths, 1869-1938 & Deaths Overseas, 1939-1947. Ancestry.com. Provo, UT, USA: Ancestry.com Operations, Inc., 2010

[4] 1901 Canada Census for Toronto, Ontario, Canada; Page 12, Line 8

[5] Death Record of John P. Keating, 1 October 1928, Ontario, Canada, Deaths, 1869-1938 & Deaths Overseas, 1939-1947. Ancestry.com. Provo, UT, USA: Ancestry.com Operations, Inc., 2010

[6] Death Record of Ann T. Adams, 9 January 1929, Ontario, Canada, Deaths, 1869-1938 & Deaths Overseas, 1939-1947. Ancestry.com. Provo, UT, USA: Ancestry.com Operations, Inc., 2010

[7] 1901 Canada Census for Toronto, Ontario, Canada; Page 3, Line 34

[8] Death Record of William Keating, 18 February 1924, Ontario, Canada, Deaths, 1869-1938 & Deaths Overseas, 1939-1947. Ancestry.com. Provo, UT, USA: Ancestry.com Operations, Inc., 2010

[9] 1901 Canada Census for Toronto, Ontario, Canada; Page 3, Line 35

[10] 1901 Canada Census for Toronto, Ontario, Canada; Page 5, Line 11

[11] 1871 Canada Census for West Garafraxa Township, Wellington County, Ontario, Canada; Pages 26-27, Lines 12-1

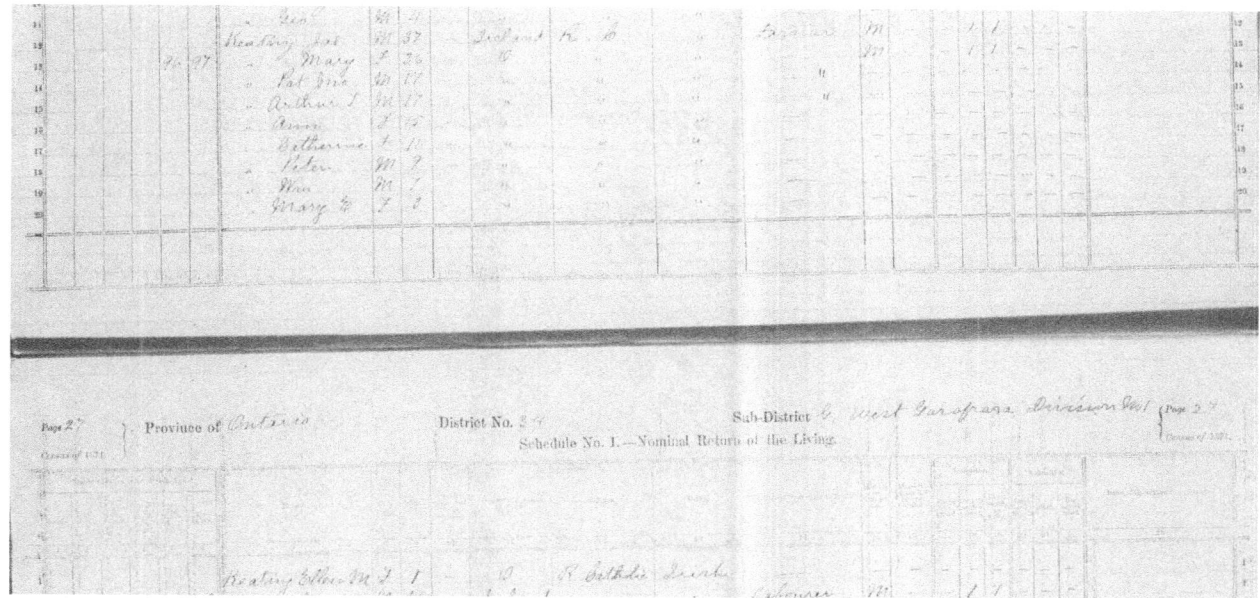

Fig.2. 1871 Canada Census for West Garafraxa Township, Wellington County, Ontario, Canada listing James Keating and Family

Death of Mary Keating

Mary Keating died between the years 1871-72 in West Garafraxa Township of unknown causes. She was buried in Marymount Cemetery (Section E) in Guelph.

Marriage to Margaret Cantwell

Margaret Cantwell was born in about 1842 in Ireland. She was residing in Arthur, Wellington County during the time she met James Keating. They were married on Tuesday, 4 November 1873 in Arthur.[12]

---

[12] Marriage Record of James Keating, 4 November 1873, Ontario, Canada, Marriages, 1801-1928. Ancestry.com. Provo, UT, USA: Ancestry.com Operations, Inc., 2010

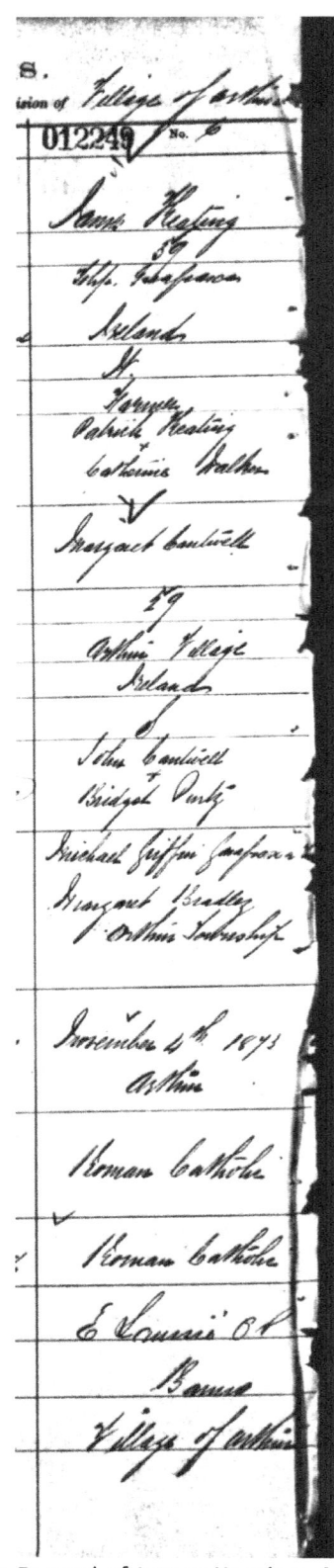

Fig.3. Marriage Record of James Keating, 4 November 1873

The couple had five children who were all born in Arthur. They were:

Alice Bridget born on Wednesday, 26 August 1874 and died on Wednesday, 1 February 1950;
Margaret born on Wednesday, 26 July 1876 and died on Tuesday, 15 February 1955;
Agnes born on Saturday, 28 December 1878 and died in 1940;
James Joseph born on Sunday, 8 August 1880;
Edward Joseph born on Thursday, 9 July 1885.

According to the 1881 Canada Census for Nichol Township, Wellington County, James Keating is listed as being 46 years of age and working as a farmer and his wife Margaret is 40 years of age with the following children: Mary age 13; Ellen age 11; Bridget age 8; Margaret age 5; Agnes age 2; James age 8 months and William age 16.[13]

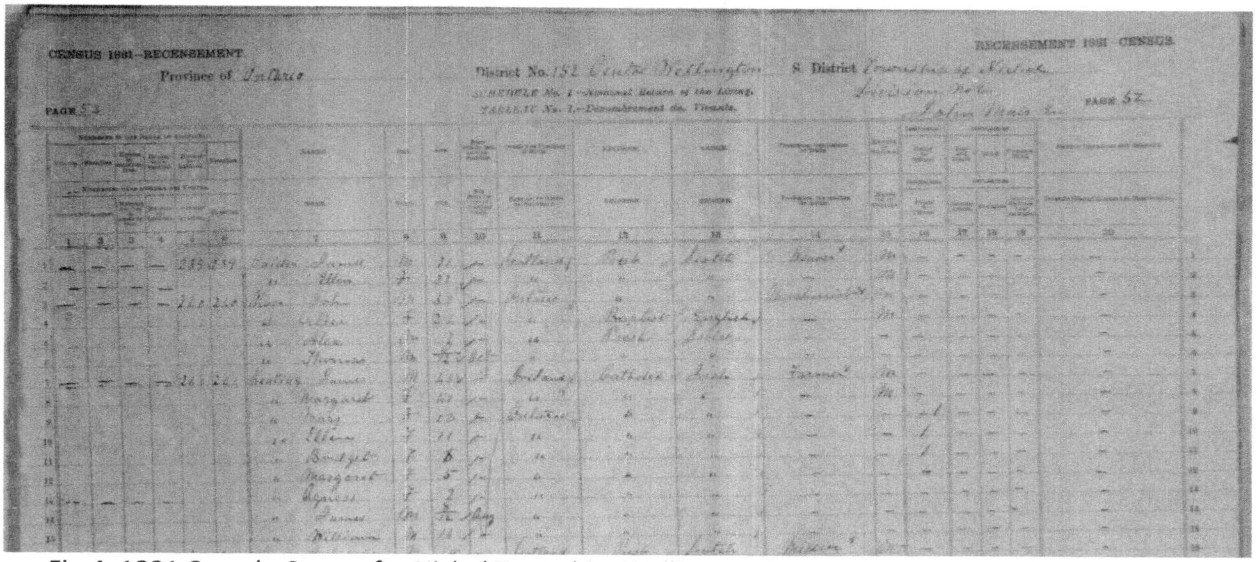
CENSUS 1881—RECENSEMENT

Province of Ontario

District No. 152 Centre Wellington

RECENSEMENT 1881 CENSUS

Fig.4. 1881 Canada Census for Nichol Township, Wellington County, Ontario, Canada listing James Keating and Family

In 1896 the family is residing in Arthur on Concession 1, Lot 8.[14]

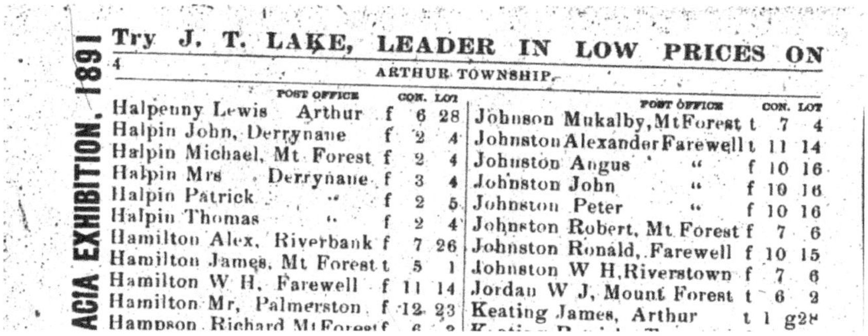
Try J. T. LAKE, LEADER IN LOW PRICES ON

4 ARTHUR TOWNSHIP.

	POST OFFICE		CON.	LOT		POST OFFICE		CON.	LOT
Halpenny Lewis	Arthur	f	6	28	Johnson Mukalby,	Mt Forest	t	7	4
Halpin John,	Derrynane	f	2	4	Johnston Alexander	Farewell	t	11	14
Halpin Michael,	Mt Forest	f	2	4	Johnston Angus	"	f	10	16
Halpin Mrs	Derrynane	f	3	4	Johnston John	"	f	10	16
Halpin Patrick	"	f	2	5	Johnston Peter	"	f	10	16
Halpin Thomas	"	f	2	4	Johnston Robert,	Mt Forest	f	7	6
Hamilton Alex,	Riverbank	f	7	26	Johnston Ronald,	Farewell	f	10	15
Hamilton James,	Mt Forest	t	5	1	Johnston W H,	Riverstown	f	7	6
Hamilton W H,	Farewell	f	11	14	Jordan W J,	Mount Forest	t	6	2
Hamilton Mr,	Palmerston	f	12	23	Keating James,	Arthur	t	1	g28

ACIA EXHIBITION, 1891

Fig.5. 1896 Farmers and Business Directory for the County of Wellington listing James Keating

---

13 1881 Canada Census for Nichol Township, Wellington County, Ontario, Canada; Page 52, Lines 7-15

14 *Farmers and Business Directory for the County of Wellington*, 1867-1900. Canadian City & Area Directories, 1819-1906. Ancestry.com. Provo, UT, USA: Ancestry.com Operations, Inc., 2010

In the 1901 Canada Census for Arthur, Wellington County, James is listed as being 65 years of age and working as a farmer and his wife Margaret is also 65 [sic] years of age with the following children: Margaret age 24; Agnes age 21; Joseph age 20 and Edward age 15.[15]

Fig.6. James and Margaret Keating and Family (Children not known in photograph) taken sometime before 1901, Photograph Courtesy of Michael T. Tracy © 2010 Michael T. Tracy

Toronto, Ontario

James and Margaret Keating and some of their family relocated to Toronto sometime after 1901. They resided at 124 Euclid Avenue.[16]

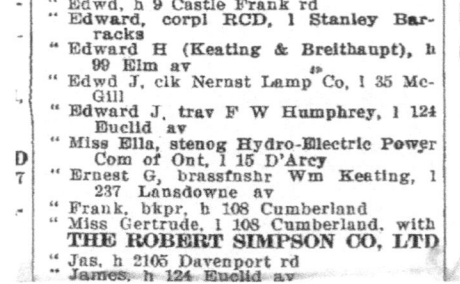

Fig.7. 1911 Toronto City Directory listing James Keating

---

[15] 1901 Canada Census for Arthur, Wellington County, Ontario, Canada; Page 11, Lines 25-30

[16] 1911 Toronto City Directory, p. 782, Toronto Public Library, Toronto, Ontario, Canada

Death of James Keating

A little over a day before his death James suffered a broken rib. On Friday, 25 August 1911 James Keating died as a result of traumatic pneumonia at the age of 77 at his home.[17]

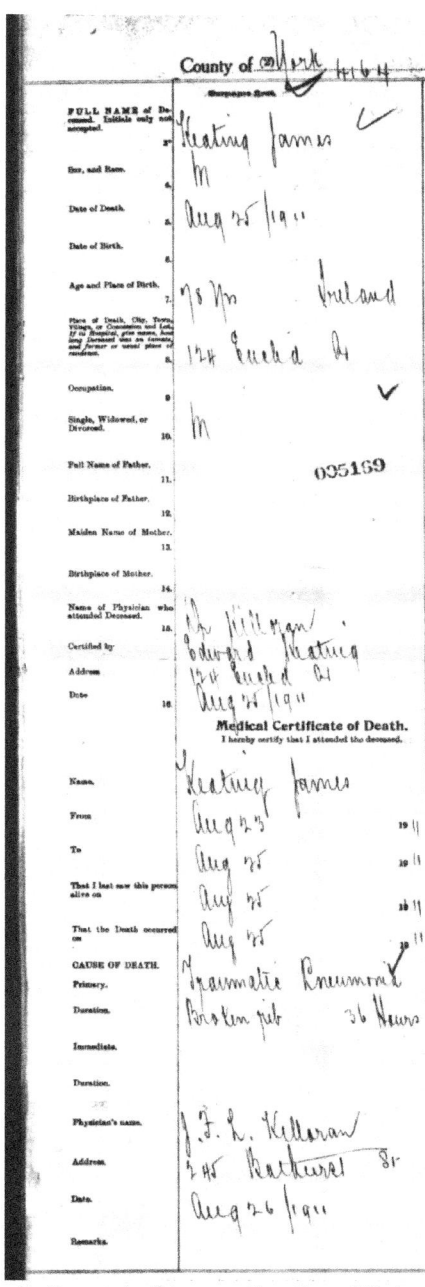

Fig.8. Death Record of James Keating, 25 August 1911

---

[17] Death Record of James Keating, 25 August 1911, Ontario, Canada, Deaths, 1869-1938 & Deaths Overseas, 1939-1947. Ancestry.com. Provo, UT, USA: Ancestry.com Operations, Inc., 2010

His death notice was published in the *Toronto World Newspaper* for Saturday, 26 August 1911: "At his residence, 124 Euclid Avenue, James Keating, in his 78th [sic] year. Funeral Monday morning at 8:45 to St. Francis Church thence to Mount Hope Cemetery. Fergus and Arthur papers please copy."[18]

Death of Margaret Keating

After the death of her husband Margaret resided with her son Edward. They resided at 473 Dovercourt Road in Toronto. Margaret died on Saturday, 17 November 1923 of senility at the age of 81.[19]

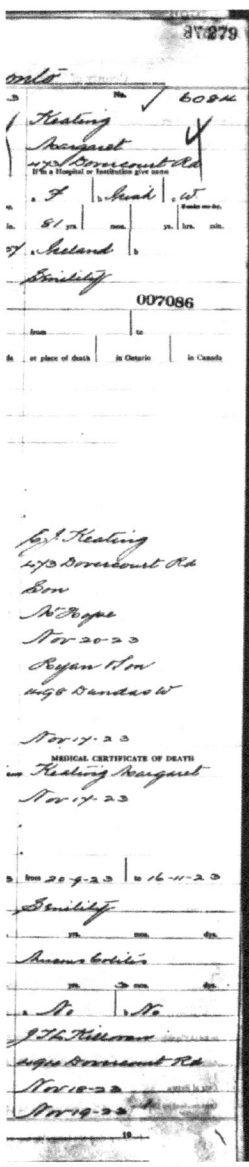

Fig.9. Death Record of Margaret Keating 17 November 1923

---

[18] *Toronto World Newspaper*, 26 August 1911 p. 7

[19] Death Record of Margaret Keating, 17 November 1923, Ontario, Canada, Deaths, 1869-1938 & Deaths Overseas, 1939-1947. Ancestry.com. Provo, UT, USA: Ancestry.com Operations, Inc., 2010

She was buried next to her husband in Mount Hope Cemetery on Monday, 19 November 1923 in Toronto.

Fig.10. Graves of James and Margaret Keating, Mount Hope Cemetery, Toronto, Ontario, Canada, Photograph Courtesy of Michael T. Tracy © 2010 Michael T. Tracy

James Keating is warmly commemorated in grateful esteem and recognition by his second great grand-nephew, Michael T. Tracy. This work is dedicated to the Memory of James Keating.

Memoratus in aeternum (Forever Remembered)

Copyright © 2016 Michael T. Tracy

John Keating (1835-): A Tribute to His Life and Times
By His Second Great Grand Nephew, Michael T. Tracy

John Keating was the fourth child of Patrick Keating and Catherine Ann Walker born in 1835 in Offaly County, Ireland. He traveled with his parents and siblings to Canada in 1837-38. He was listed in the 1851 Canada Census for Pilkington Township, Wellington County, Ontario, Canada as being 16 years of age and working as a farmer.[1]

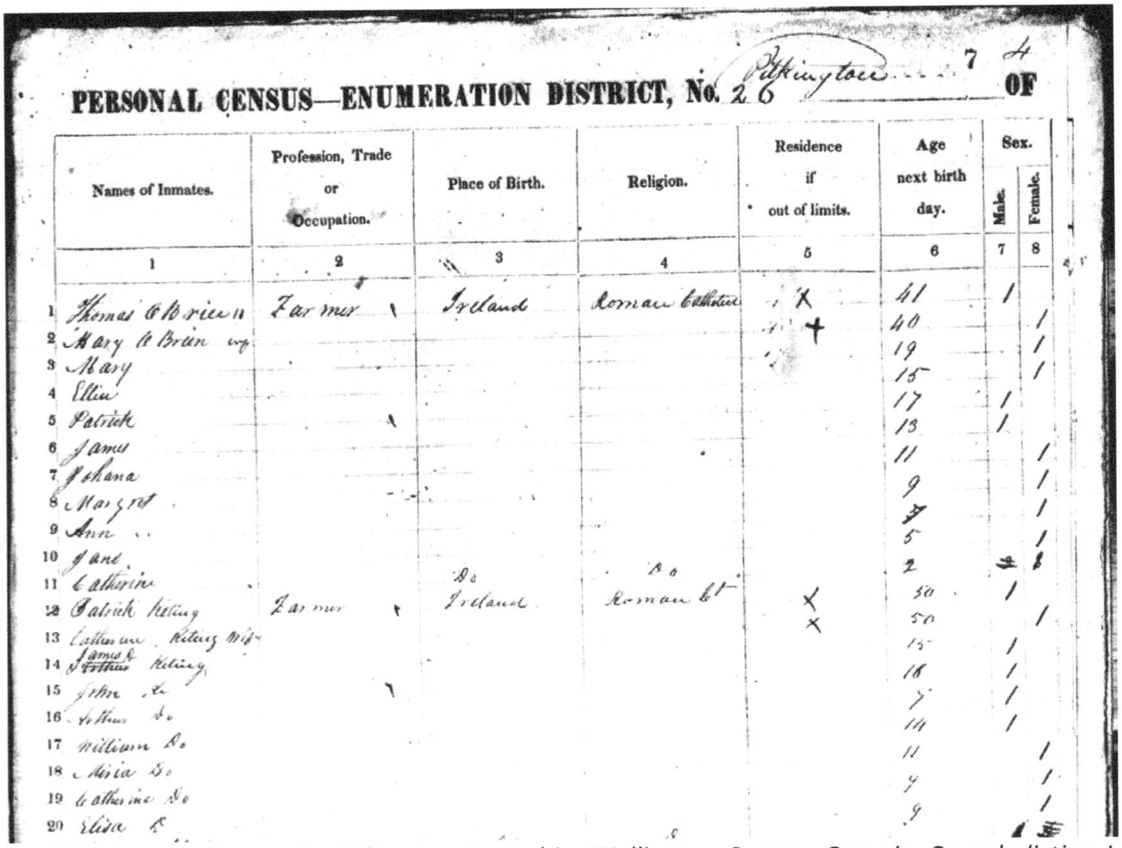

Fig.1. 1851 Canada Census for Pilkington Township, Wellington County, Ontario, Canada listing John Keating

It is not known exactly when John Keating died except that it was between the years of 1851-61.

John Keating is warmly commemorated in grateful esteem and recognition by his second great grand-nephew, Michael T. Tracy.

Memoratus in aeternum (Forever Remembered)

Copyright © 2016 Michael T. Tracy

---

[1] 1851 Canada Census for Pilkington Township, Wellington County, Ontario, Canada; Page 7, Line 15

Arthur Keating (1837-1917): A Tribute to his Life and Times
By His Second Great Grand Nephew, Michael T. Tracy

Arthur Keating was the last child of Patrick Keating and Catherine Ann Walker born in Offaly County, Ireland. As an infant he, along with his parents and siblings, would cross the Atlantic Ocean to Canada and the promise it held to these Irish immigrants. Like his father before him, Keating would farm his lands residing in West Garafraxa Township for most of his life. He was considered to be one of the old pioneers of West Garafraxa having resided in the township for over sixty-five years, and fifty years on his farm located at Lot 20, Concession 2. Arthur would marry and have nine children who were all born in West Garafraxa Township. This then is the narrative of the life and times of Arthur Keating.

Early years

Arthur Keating was born on Thursday, 15 June 1837 in Eglish Parish, Kings County, presently called Offaly County, Ireland.[1] In 1837-38 he left Ireland with his parents and siblings and traveled to Ontario, Canada settling in Pilkington Township, Wellington County. He is listed in the 1851 Canada Census for Pilkington Township, Wellington County as being 7 [sic] years of age.[2]

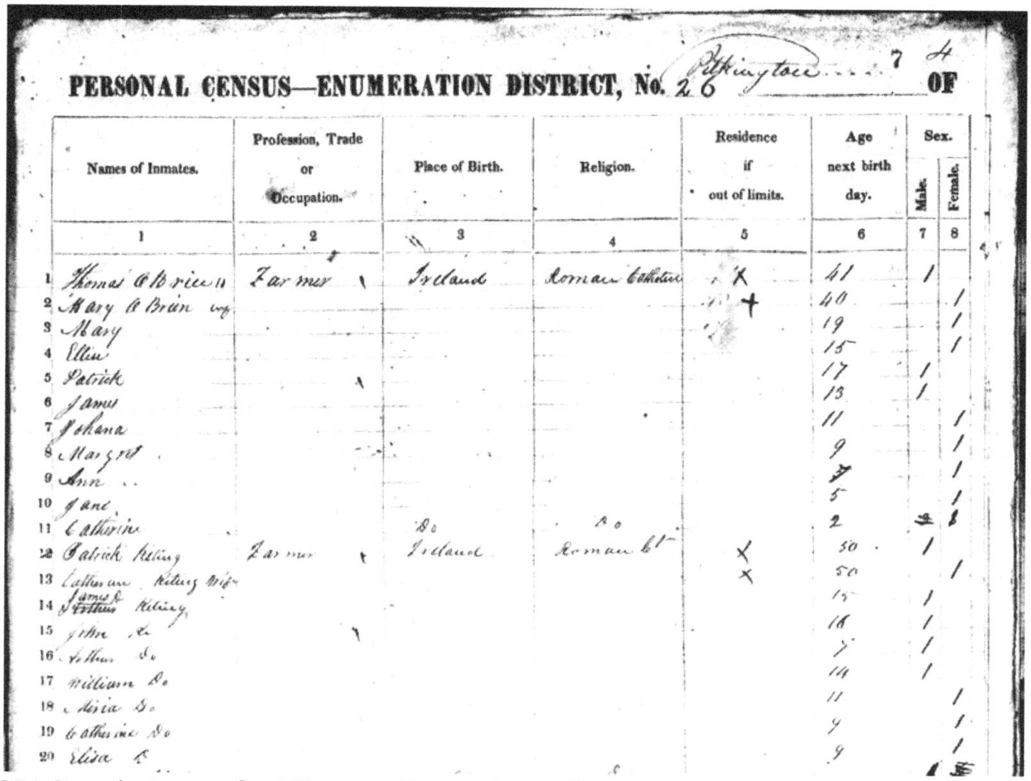

PERSONAL CENSUS—ENUMERATION DISTRICT, No. 26 Pilkington 7 4 OF

	Names of Inmates.	Profession, Trade or Occupation.	Place of Birth.	Religion.	Residence if out of limits.	Age next birth day.	Sex. Male.	Sex. Female.
	1	2	3	4	5	6	7	8
1	Thomas O'Brien	Farmer	Ireland	Roman Catholic	X	41	1	
2	Mary O'Brien wife				+	40		1
3	Mary					19		1
4	Ellen					15		1
5	Patrick					17	1	
6	James					13	1	
7	Johana					11		1
8	Margret					9		1
9	Ann					7		1
10	Jane					5		1
11	Catherine		Do	Do		2		1
12	Patrick Keting	Farmer	Ireland	Roman Ct	X	50	1	
13	Catherine Keting Wife				X	50		1
14	James & ~~Arthur~~ Keting					15	1	
15	John Do					16	1	
16	Arthur Do					7	1	
17	William Do					14	1	
18	Maria Do					11		1
19	Catherine Do					9		1
20	Eliza Do					9		1

Fig.1. 1851 Canada Census for Pilkington Township, Wellington County, Ontario, Canada listing Arthur Keating

---

1 1901 Canada Census for West Garafraxa Township, Wellington County, Ontario, Canada; Page 4, Line 38

2 1851 Canada Census for Pilkington Township, Wellington County, Ontario, Canada; Page 7, Line 16

Marriage and Family life

Arthur Keating met and later married Ann Daly on Tuesday, 1 February 1859 in Guelph by the Reverend John Holzer and the witnesses to the marriage were recorded as Thomas Corbett and his sister Maria Keating.[3] Arthur and Ann Keating had nine children who were all born in West Garafraxa Township. They were:

Catherine born on Friday, 30 September 1859[4] and died on Sunday, 29 July 1883;[5]
James born on Thursday, 7 November 1861[6] and died on Thursday, 6 July 1933;[7]
Mary Elizabeth born on Sunday, 4 September 1864[8] and died on Wednesday, 15 February 1899;[9]
John Patrick born on Monday, 18 September 1865 and died on Saturday, 13 September 1924;[10]
Peter born in 1869 and died on Saturday, 1 January 1944;[11]
Thomas A. born on Friday, 17 October 1873 and died on Saturday, 7 January 1939;[12]
Arthur born on Monday, 21 June 1875 and died on Sunday, 3 November 1918;[13]
Mary born on Monday, 27 October 1879;
Frederick William born on Sunday, 8 July 1883 and died on Thursday, 31 May 1956.

    Arthur and Ann resided on Lot 20, Concession 2 for most of their lives having purchased the 100-acre property in 1867.

---

[3] Marriage Record of Arthur Keating, 1 February 1859, Ontario, Canada, Marriages, 1801-1928. Ancestry.com. Provo, UT, USA: Ancestry.com Operations, Inc., 2010

[4] Baptismal Record of Catherine Keating, 7 October 1859, Church of Our Lady Records, Guelph, Ontario, Canada

[5] Death Record of Catherine Heffernan, 29 July 1883, Ontario, Canada, Deaths, 1869-1938 & Deaths Overseas, 1939-1947. Ancestry.com. Provo, UT, USA: Ancestry.com Operations, Inc., 2010

[6] Baptismal Record of James Keating, 15 December 1861, Church of Our Lady Records, Guelph, Ontario, Canada

[7] Death Record of James Keating, 6 July 1933, Ontario, Canada, Deaths, 1869-1938 & Deaths Overseas, 1939-1947. Ancestry.com. Provo, UT, USA: Ancestry.com Operations, Inc., 2010

[8] Baptismal Record of Mary Elizabeth Keating, 6 March 1865, Church of Our Lady Records, Guelph, Ontario, Canada

[9] Death Record of Mary E. Griffin, 15 February 1899, Ontario, Canada, Deaths, 1869-1938 & Deaths Overseas, 1939-1947. Ancestry.com. Provo, UT, USA: Ancestry.com Operations, Inc., 2010

[10] Death Record of John P. Keating, 13 September 1924, Cook County, Illinois Death Index, 1908-1988. Ancestry.com. Provo, UT, USA: Ancestry.com Operations, Inc., 2008

[11] Death Record of Peter Keating, 1 January 1944, Illinois, Deaths & Stillbirths Index, 1916-1947. Ancestry.com. Provo, UT, USA: Ancestry.com Operations, Inc., 2011

[12] Thomas A. Keating Obituary, *The Garfieldian Newspaper*, 19 January 1939 p. 9

[13] Death Record of Arthur Keating, 3 November 1918, Illinois, Cook County Deaths, 1878-1922. Index and Images. Family Search, 2010

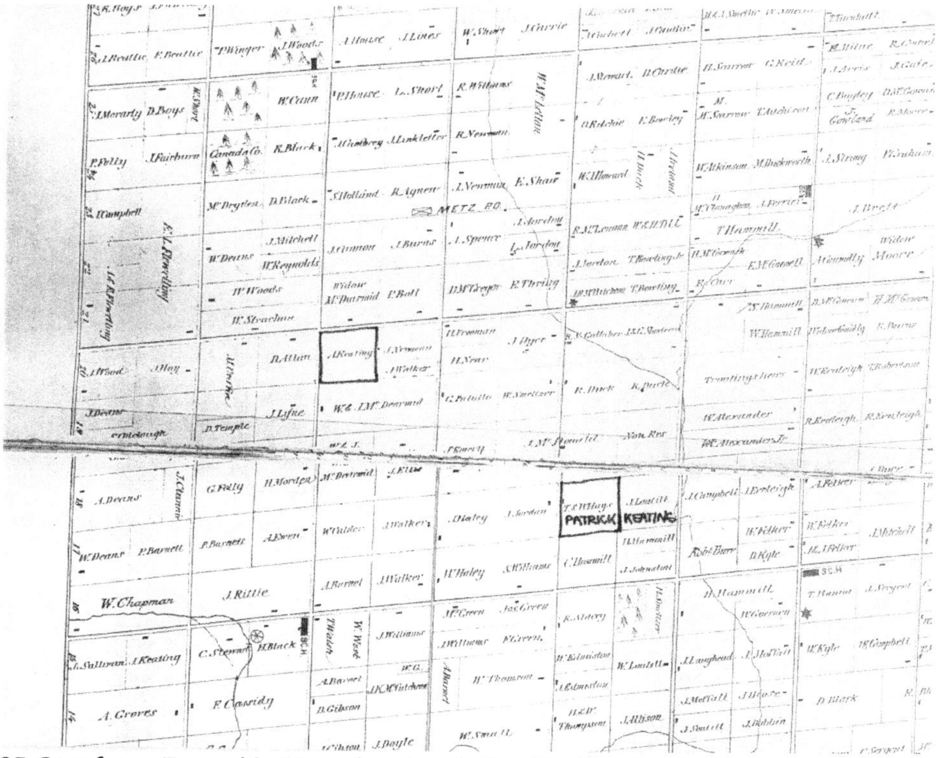

Fig.2. 1885 Garafraxa Township Map showing Arthur Keating lands, Photograph Courtesy of the Wellington County Museum and Archives

The Keating family is listed in the 1871 Canada Census for West Garafraxa Township which listed Arthur as being 35 years of age, born in Ireland and working as a farmer and Ann is 33 years of age with the following children: Catherine age 11; Elizabeth age 9; John age 7; James age 5 and Peter age 3.[14]

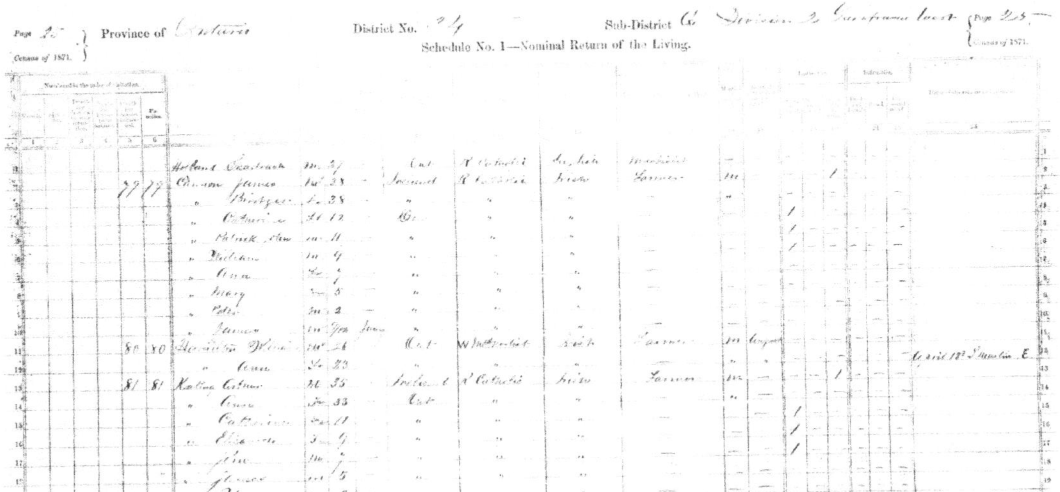
Page 25 Census of 1871. Province of Ontario District No. 24 Sub-District G Division 2 Garafraxa West Page 25 Census of 1871.
Schedule No. 1—Nominal Return of the Living.

Fig.3. 1871 Canada Census for West Garafraxa Township, Wellington County, Ontario, Canada listing Arthur Keating and Family

14 1871 Canada Census for West Garafraxa Township, Wellington County, Ontario, Canada; Page 25, Lines 13-19

The Keating family is listed in the 1881 Canada Census for West Garafraxa Township showing Arthur as being 45 years of age and working as a farmer and his wife Ann is 42 years of age with the following children: Catherine age 20; Elizabeth age 18; John age 16; James age 14; Peter age 12; Arthur age 9; Thomas age 7 and Mary age 4.[15]

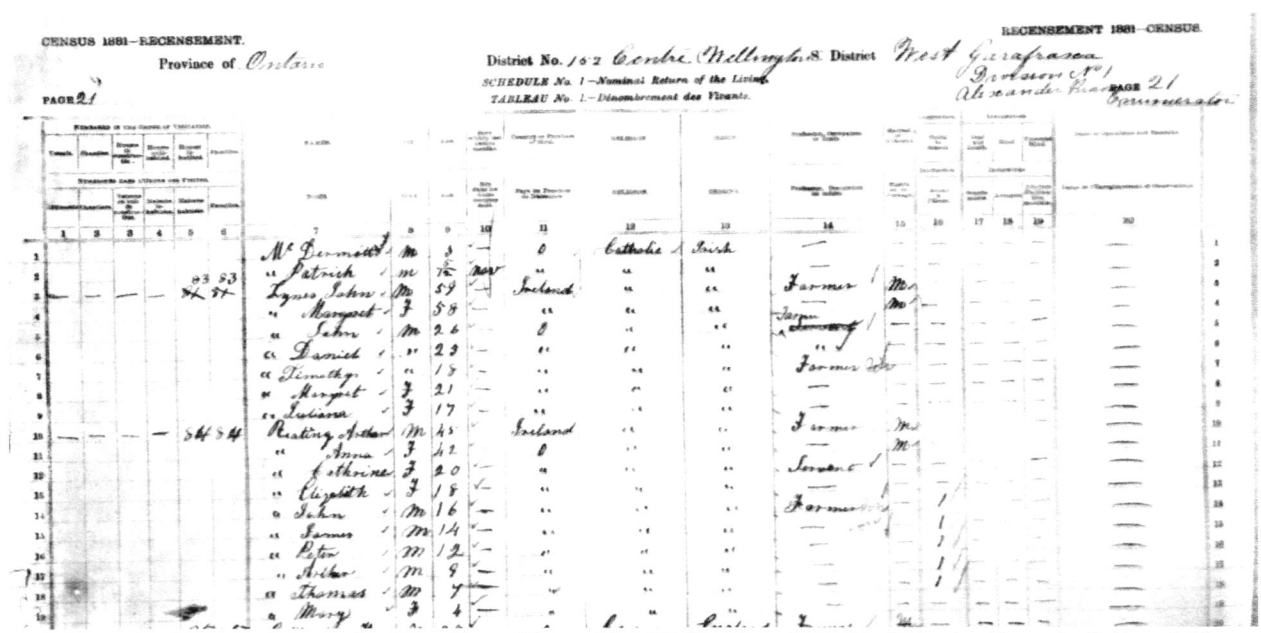

Fig.4. 1881 Canada Census for Garafraxa Township, Wellington County, Ontario, Canada listing Arthur Keating and Family

According to the 1891 Canada Census for West Garafraxa Township Arthur is listed as being 55 years of age and working as a farmer and his wife Ann is 53 years of age with the following children: Arthur age 19; Thomas age 17; Mary age 13 and Frederick age 8.[16]

---

[15] 1881 Canada Census for West Garafraxa Township, Wellington County, Ontario, Canada; Page 21, Lines 10-19
[16] 1891 Canada Census for West Garafraxa Township, Wellington County, Ontario, Canada; Page 9, Lines 17-22

Fig.5. 1891 Canada Census for West Garafraxa Township, Wellington County, Ontario, Canada listing Arthur Keating and Family

By 1901 Arthur Keating is listed in the Census as being 63 years of age and working as a farmer and his wife Ann is listed as being 59 years of age with the following children: Mary (Minnie) age 22 and Frederick age 18.[17]

Fig.6. 1901 Canada Census for West Garafraxa Township, Wellington County, Ontario, Canada listing Arthur Keating and Family

Arthur Keating is listed in the 1911 Canada Census for West Garafraxa Township as being 75 years of age and his wife Ann is 73 years of age with the following children: Mary age 32 and Frederick age 28 and working as a farmer.[18]

---

[17] 1901 Canada Census for West Garafraxa Township, Wellington County, Ontario, Canada; Page 4, Lines 38-41

[18] 1911 Canada Census for West Garafraxa Township, Wellington County, Ontario, Canada; Page 4, Lines 25-30

Fig.7. 1911 Canada Census for West Garafraxa Township, Wellington County, Ontario, Canada listing Arthur Keating and Family

Fig.8. Arthur Keating, unknown date, Photograph Courtesy of Michael T. Tracy © 2010 Michael T. Tracy

Death of Arthur Keating

Arthur Keating died on Wednesday, 21 February 1917 at his residence in West Garafraxa at the age of 79 of senile decay.[19]

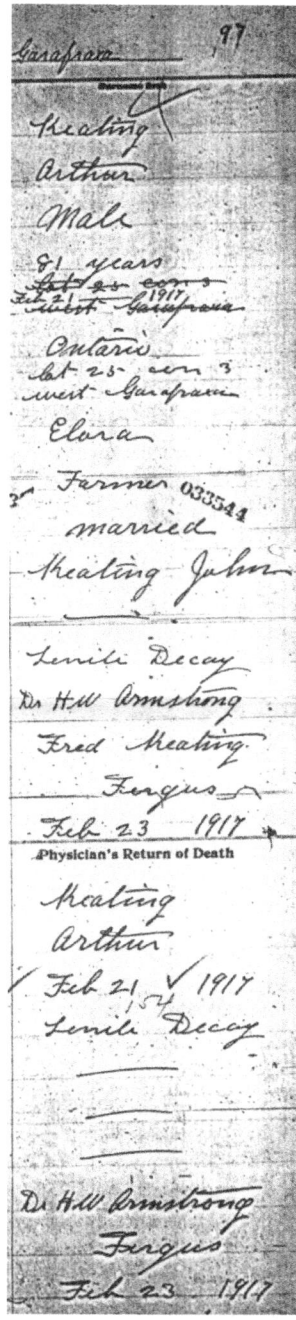

Fig.9. Death Record of Arthur Keating, 21 February 1917

---

[19] Death Record of Arthur Keating, 21 February 1917, Ontario, Canada, Deaths, 1869-1938 & Deaths Overseas, 1939-1947. Ancestry.com. Provo, UT, USA: Ancestry.com Operations, Inc., 2010

His obituary notices were published in the *Fergus News Record Newspaper* dated Thursday, 22 February 1917 which are reprinted below.

DEATHS.

KEATING—In West Garafraxa, on Wednesday, Feb. 21st, 1917, Arthur Keating, aged 81 years. Funeral will leave his late residence, lot 20, con. 2, West Gara., on Saturday, Feb. 24th, at 9.30 a.m., for the R.C. cemetery, Elora.

Fig.10. Arthur Keating Obituary Notice, Fergus News Record, 22 February 1917

DEATH OF MR. ARTHUR KEATING.

It is with much regret that we announce the death of one of the old pioneers of West Garafraxa, in the person of Mr. Arthur Keating, on Wednesday, February 21st, 1917, at the age of 81 years. He had lived in the township for over sixty-five years, and fifty years on the farm on which he died.

The funeral, which was held on Saturday to the R.C. cemetery, Elora, was largely attended by friends and relatives of the family, many of whom came from Toronto, Guelph, Chicago and Pittsburg. The pallbearers were his four sons, John, James, Arthur, Thomas and his nephew Mr. Wm. Keating, of Toronto, and his son-in-law, John Heffernan.

The deceased was married 56 years ago to Ann Daly, of Nichol township, who survives him, with six sons and one daughter, John, James, Peter, Arthur and Thomas all of Chicago; Frederick of the old homestead, and Mrs. John Heffernan, of Luther.

Fig.11. Arthur Keating Obituary Notice, Fergus News Record, 26 February 1917

He was buried on Saturday, 24 February 1917 at St. Mary Immaculate Cemetery (Section D, Row 10-2) in Elora.

Death of Ann Keating

Ann Keating died on Saturday, 13 September 1919 at the age of 81 of senility in West Luther Township, Wellington County.[20]

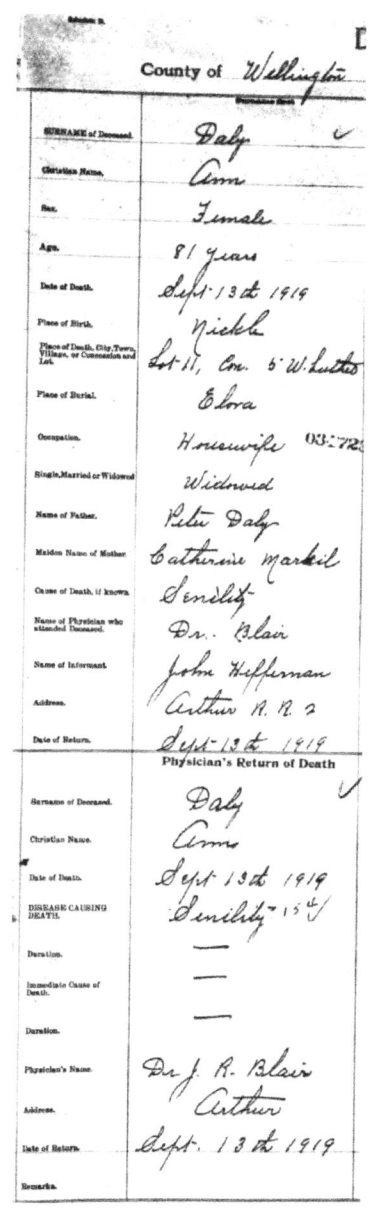

Fig.12. Death Record of Ann Keating, 13 September 1919

---

[20] Death Record of Ann Keating, 13 September 1919, Ontario, Canada, Deaths, 1869-1938 & Deaths Overseas, 1939-1947. Ancestry.com. Provo, UT, USA: Ancestry.com Operations, Inc., 2010

She was buried next to her husband in St. Mary Immaculate Cemetery in Elora on Tuesday, 16 September 1919.

Fig.13. Graves of Arthur and Ann Keating, St. Mary Immaculate Cemetery, Elora, Ontario, Canada, Photograph Courtesy of Michael T. Tracy © 2010 Michael T. Tracy

Arthur Keating is warmly commemorated in grateful esteem and recognition by his second great grand-nephew, Michael T. Tracy. This work is dedicated to the Memory of Arthur Keating.

Memoratus in aeternum (Forever Remembered)

Copyright © 2016 Michael T. Tracy

Mariah (Maria) (Keating) Corbett (1838-1914): A Tribute to Her Life and Times
By Her Second Great Grandson, Michael T. Tracy

Mariah (Maria) Keating was the first child of Patrick Keating and Catherine Ann Walker to be born in Canada. The family had left Kings County, presently called Offaly County, Ireland no more than two years before her birth. Maria would grow up in Pilkington and Garafraxa Townships, Wellington County, Ontario.

Fig.1. Residence of Patrick and Catherine Keating, West Garafraxa Township, Wellington County, Ontario, Canada, Photograph Courtesy of Michael T. Tracy © 2010 Michael T. Tracy

She would meet and later marry Thomas Corbett and they would have ten children eventually residing in Fergus. Thomas would run two hotels: the Elgin Hotel and the Queen's Arms Hotel. By 1882 the family left Canada and resided in Chicago, Illinois. Thomas Corbett worked in the Union Stock Yards as a carpenter. The couple celebrated their Golden Wedding Anniversary on Sunday, 21 November 1909 with their entire family and friends present. This then is the narrative of the life and times of Mariah (Maria) (Keating) Corbett.

Early years

Mariah (Maria) Keating was born in November of 1838 in Pilkington Township, Wellington County, Ontario, Canada.[1] She was the sixth child born to Patrick Keating, a farmer, and Catherine Ann Walker. She is listed in the 1851 Canada Census for Pilkington Township, Wellington County, Ontario, Canada

---

[1] Death Record of Mariah Corbett, 13 August 1914, Illinois, Cook County Deaths, 1878-1922. Index and Images. Family Search, 2010

as being 11 years of age.[2]

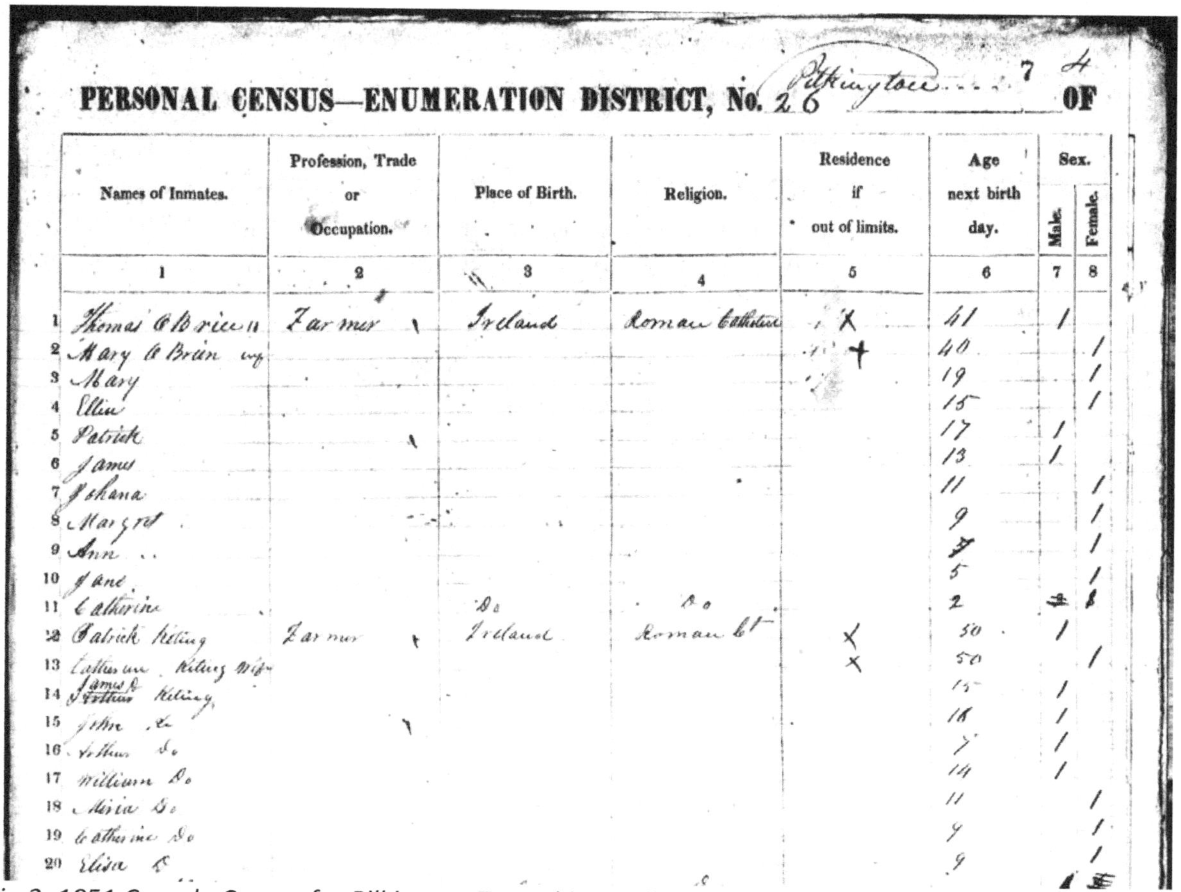

PERSONAL CENSUS—ENUMERATION DISTRICT, No. 26 Pilkington 7 4 OF

	Names of Inmates.	Profession, Trade or Occupation.	Place of Birth.	Religion.	Residence if out of limits.	Age next birth day.	Sex. Male.	Sex. Female.
	1	2	3	4	5	6	7	8
1	Thomas O'Brien	Farmer	Ireland	Roman Catholic	X	41	1	
2	Mary O'Brien wife				+	40		1
3	Mary					19		1
4	Ellen					15		1
5	Patrick					17	1	
6	James					13	1	
7	Johana					11		1
8	Margret					9		1
9	Ann					7		1
10	Jane					5		1
11	Catherine		Do	Do		2		1
12	Patrick Keling	Farmer	Ireland	Roman Ct	X	50	1	
13	Catherine Keling wife				X	50		1
14	James & Arthur Keling					15	1	
15	John Do					16	1	
16	Arthur Do					7	1	
17	William Do					14	1	
18	Maria Do					11		1
19	Catherine Do					9		1
20	Elisa Do					9		1

Fig.2. 1851 Canada Census for Pilkington Township, Wellington County, Ontario, Canada listing Maria Keating (Line 18)

Marriage and Family life

Maria met Thomas Corbett, a farmer, sometime in the late 1850s. They were married on Tuesday, 22 November 1859 at the Church of Our Lady Immaculate in Guelph.[3] As a wedding present the couple, were given plates and saucers which have been in the family for generations.

---

[2] 1851 Canada Census for Pilkington Township, Wellington County, Ontario, Canada; Page 7, Line 18

[3] Marriage Record of Maria Keating, 22 November 1859, Ontario, Canada, Marriages, 1801-1928. Ancestry.com. Provo, UT, USA: Ancestry.com Operations, Inc., 2010

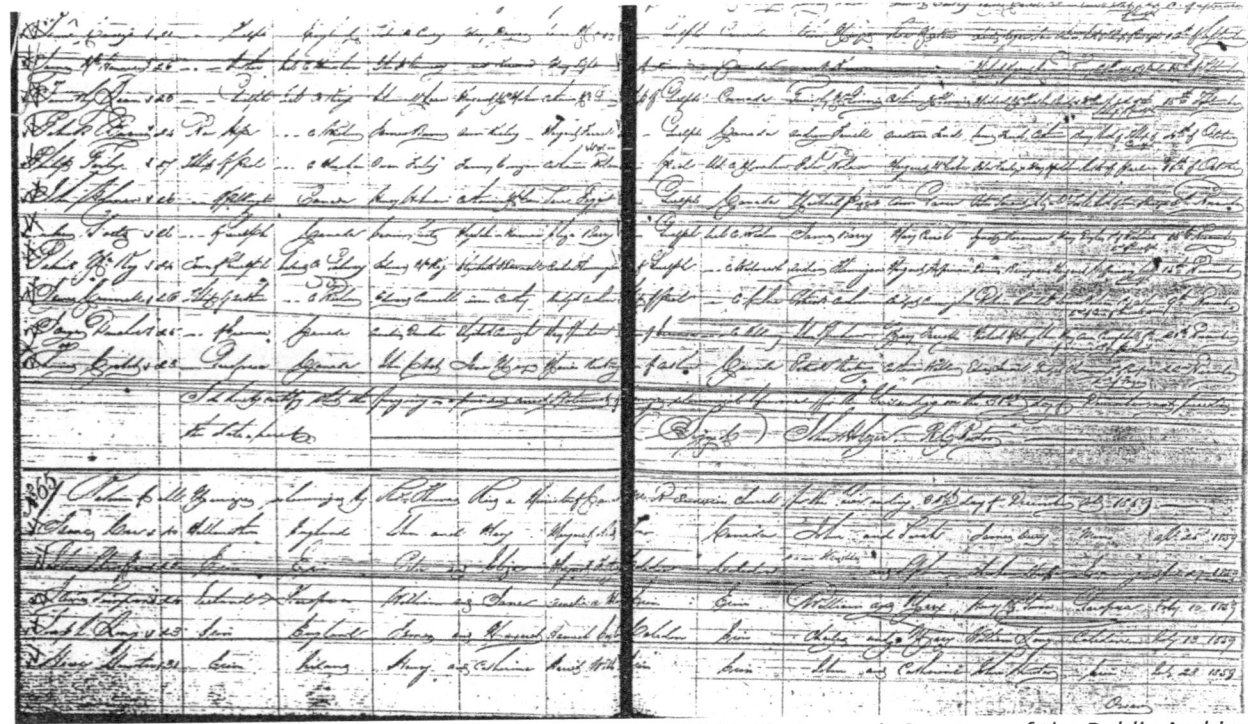

Fig.3. Marriage Record of Maria Keating, 22 November 1859, Photograph Courtesy of the Public Archives of Canada

An interesting story was published fifty years later in the *Chicago Daily Newspaper* on Tuesday, 23 November 1909 concerning an event before their wedding: "Mr. Corbett was born in 1833 and married Maria Keating in Toronto [sic] in 1859 after a tragedy in which another Canadian lost his life. The man who met death was Mr. Corbett's rival and thought Miss Keating was in danger of drowning. In attempting to save her he was drowned. It developed afterward that the woman who was rescued was not Miss Keating."[4]

Fig.4. Wedding Plate of Thomas and Maria Corbett, 22 November 1859, Photograph Courtesy of Michael T. Tracy © 2010 Michael T. Tracy

---

[4] *Chicago Daily Newspaper*, 23 November 1909

The couple had ten children. They were:

John born on Tuesday, 20 November 1860;[5]
Arthur J., born on Friday, 28 February 1862[6] and died on Monday, 6 November 1911;[7]
Elizabeth (Leah) born on Tuesday, 19 May 1863[8] and died on Friday, 14 November 1941;[9]
Anna Catherine born on Saturday, 6 July 1867[10] and died on Sunday, 10 October 1948;[11]
William born on Tuesday, 21 April 1868[12] and died on Saturday, 31 January 1925;[13]
Albert Edwin born on Monday, 28 November 1870[14] and died on Wednesday, 24 March 1943;[15]
Thomas Lee born on Sunday, 29 October 1871[16] and died on Tuesday, 3 May 1938;[17]
Albina born on Thursday, 16 August 1872[18] and died on Saturday, 16 October 1875;[19]
Alfred John born on Monday, 20 September 1874[20] and died on Wednesday, 14 March 1951;[21]
Maud (Maria) Dimpna born on Tuesday, 8 February 1876[22] and died on Saturday, 4 January 1890.[23]

According to the 1861 Canada Census for Garafraxa Township, Wellington County Thomas Corbett is listed as being 27 years of age and working as a laborer and residing in a log house; his wife Maria is 20 years old with the following child: John age 7 months.[24]

---

[5] Baptismal Record of John Corbett, 2 December 1860, Church of Our Lady Immaculate Baptismal Records, Guelph, Ontario, Canada

[6] Baptismal Record of Arthur Corbett, 23 March 1862, Church of Our Lady Immaculate Baptismal Records, Guelph, Ontario, Canada

[7] Death Record of Arthur J. Corbett, 6 November 1911, Illinois, Cook County Deaths, 1878-1922. Index and Images. Family Search, 2010

[8] Baptismal Record of Elizabeth Corbett, 5 July 1863, Church of Our Lady Immaculate Baptismal Records, Guelph, Ontario, Canada

[9] Death Record of Elizabeth Murray, 14 November 1941, Cook County, Illinois Death Index, 1908-1988. Ancestry.com. Provo, UT, USA: Ancestry.com Operations, Inc., 2008

[10] Death Record of Anna C. Buist, 10 October 1948, Illinois Department of Public Health, Springfield, Illinois

[11] Death Record of Anna C. Buist, 10 October 1948, Illinois Department of Public Health, Springfield, Illinois

[12] Death Record of William Corbett, 31 January 1925, Cook County, Illinois Death Index, 1908-1988. Ancestry.com. Provo, UT, USA: Ancestry.com Operations, Inc., 2008

[13] Death Record of William Corbett, 31 January 1925, Cook County, Illinois Death Index, 1908-1988. Ancestry.com. Provo, UT, USA: Ancestry.com Operations, Inc., 2008

[14] Baptismal Record of Albert Edwin Corbett, 18 December 1870, Church of Our Lady Immaculate Baptismal Records, Guelph, Ontario, Canada

[15] Death Record of Albert E. Corbett, 24 March 1943, Cook County, Illinois Death Index, 1908-1988. Ancestry.com. Provo, UT, USA: Ancestry.com Operations, Inc., 2008

[16] Death Record of Thomas Lee Corbett, 3 May 1938, Cook County, Illinois Death Index, 1908-1988. Ancestry.com. Provo, UT, USA: Ancestry.com Operations, Inc., 2008

[17] Death Record of Thomas Lee Corbett, 3 May 1938, Cook County, Illinois Death Index, 1908-1988. Ancestry.com. Provo, UT, USA: Ancestry.com Operations, Inc., 2008

[18] Baptismal Record of Albina Corbett, 1 September 1872, St. Mary Immaculate Church Records, Elora, Ontario, Canada

[19] Death Record of Albina Corbett, 16 October 1875, Ontario, Canada, Deaths, 1869-1938 & Deaths Overseas, 1939-1947. Ancestry.com. Provo, UT, USA: Ancestry.com Operations, Inc., 2010

[20] Baptismal Record of Alfred John Corbett, 29 September 1874, St. Mary Immaculate Church Records, Elora, Ontario, Canada

[21] Death Record of Alfred J. Corbett, 14 March 1951, Cook County Clerk's Office, Chicago, Illinois

[22] Baptismal Record of Maud Dimpna Corbett, 13 February 1874, St. Mary Immaculate Church Records, Elora, Ontario, Canada

[23] Death Record of Maud D. Corbett, 4 January 1890, Illinois, Cook County Deaths, 1878-1922. Index and Images. Family Search, 2010

[24] 1861 Canada Census for Garafraxa Township, Wellington County, Ontario, Canada; Page 38, Lines 2-4

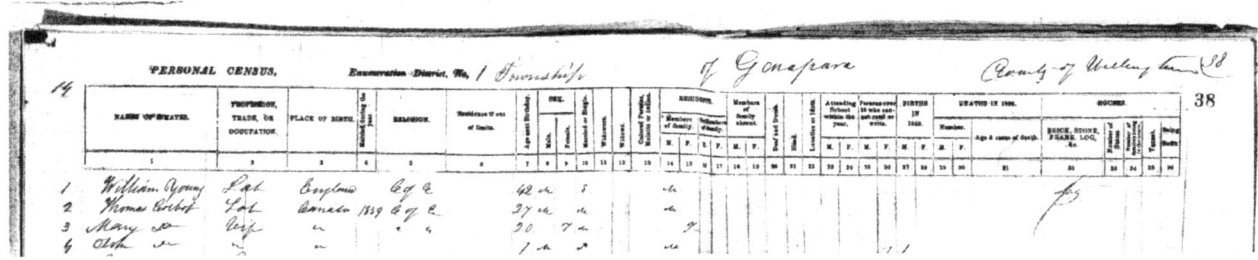

Fig.5. 1861 Canada Census for Garafraxa Township, Wellington County, Ontario, Canada listing Thomas and Maria Corbett and Family

The Corbett family is listed in the 1871 Canada Census for Fergus, Wellington County, Ontario listing Thomas as being 34 years of age and working as a tavern keeper and his wife Maria is 32 years of age with the following children: Arthur age 8; Margaret Jane [sic] Elizabeth age 6; Catherine age 5; William age 3; Thomas age 2 and Maria's sister Elizabeth Keating age 21 and working as a servant.[25]

Fig.6. 1871 Canada Census for Fergus, Wellington County, Ontario, Canada listing Thomas and Maria Corbett and Family

The family is listed in the 1881 Canada Census for Fergus with Thomas now being 46 years of age and working as an innkeeper and Maria is 44 years of age with the following children: Arthur age 19 and working as a butcher; Elizabeth age 17 and working as a tailoress; Catherine age 15; William age 14; Thomas age 12; Albert age 10; Alfred age 7 and Maria age 5.[26]

---

[25] 1871 Canada Census for Fergus, Wellington County, Ontario, Canada; Page 30, Lines 1-9
[26] 1881 Canada Census for Fergus, Wellington County, Ontario, Canada; Page 9, Lines 9-18

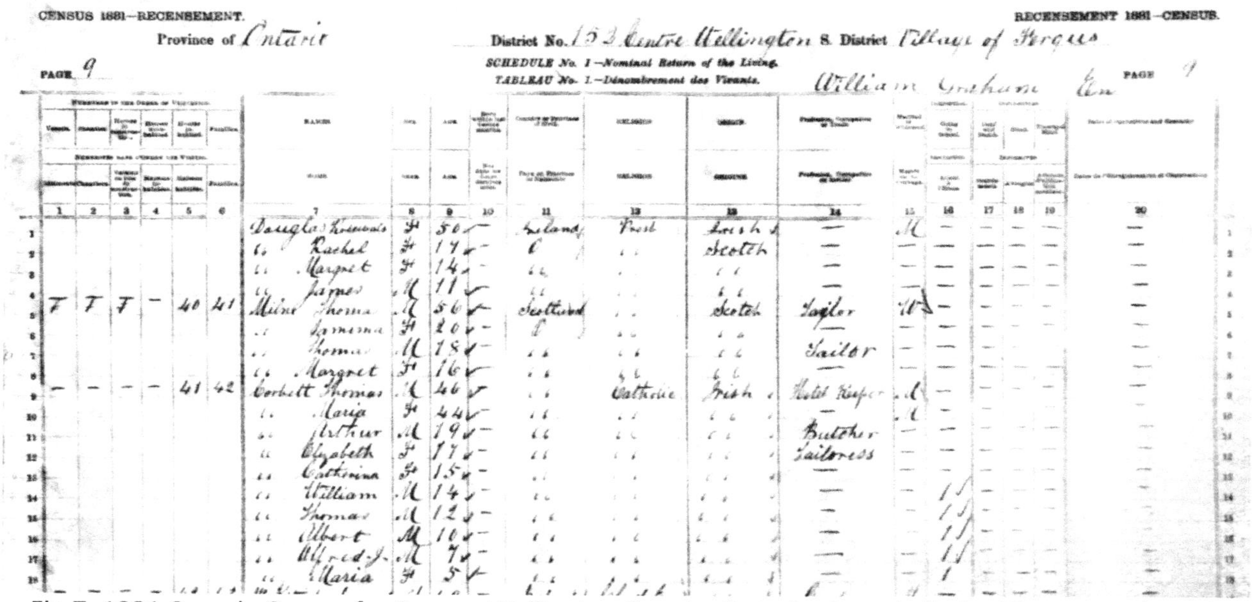

CENSUS 1881—RECENSEMENT. Province of Ontario District No. 153 Centre Wellington S. District Village of Fergus RECENSEMENT 1881—CENSUS.

PAGE 9 SCHEDULE No. 1—Nominal Return of the Living. TABLEAU No. 1—Dénombrement des Vivants. William Graham En. PAGE 9

Line	1	2	3	4	5	6	7 Names	8 Sex	9 Age	10	11 Country or Province of Birth	12 Religion	13 Origin	14 Profession, Occupation or Trade	15 Married or Widowed	16	17	18	19	20
1							Douglas Rosanna	F	50		Ireland	Presb	Irish	—	M	—	—	—	—	—
2							" Rachel	F	17		C	"	Scotch	—	—	—	—	—	—	—
3							" Margret	F	14		"	"	"	—	—	—	—	—	—	—
4							" James	M	11		"	"	"	—	—	—	—	—	—	—
5	7	7	7	—	40	41	Milne Thomas	M	56		Scotland	"	Scotch	Tailor	W	—	—	—	—	—
6							" Jemima	F	20		C	"	"	—	—	—	—	—	—	—
7							" Thomas	M	18		"	"	"	Sailor	—	—	—	—	—	—
8							" Margret	F	16		"	"	"	—	—	—	—	—	—	—
9	—	—	—	—	41	42	Corbett Thomas	M	46		"	Catholic	Irish	Hotel Keeper	M	—	—	—	—	—
10							" Maria	F	44		"	"	"	—	M	—	—	—	—	—
11							" Arthur	M	19		"	"	"	Butcher	—	—	—	—	—	—
12							" Elizabeth	F	17		"	"	"	Tailoress	—	—	—	—	—	—
13							" Catherina	F	15		"	"	"	—	—	—	—	—	—	—
14							" William	M	14		"	"	"	—	—	1	—	—	—	—
15							" Thomas	M	12		"	"	"	—	—	1	—	—	—	—
16							" Albert	M	10		"	"	"	—	—	1	—	—	—	—
17							" Alfred J.	M	7		"	"	"	—	—	1	—	—	—	—
18							" Maria	F	5		"	"	"	—	—	1	—	—	—	—

Fig.7. 1881 Canada Census for Fergus, Wellington County, Ontario, Canada listing Thomas and Maria Corbett and Family

Chicago, Illinois

By 1882 the entire Corbett family relocated to Chicago, Illinois and purchased a home located at 4815 South Atlantic Street. Thomas and Maria Corbett resided in this home until both of their deaths. Maria Corbett became a U.S. citizen along with her husband on Wednesday, 2 November 1892 at Chicago.

According to the 1900 U.S. Federal Census for Chicago, Cook County, Illinois, Thomas is 64 years of age and working as a carpenter and his wife Maria is also 64 years of age with the following children: Maud age 15 and Thomas age 29 and working as a hotel bookkeeper along with his wife Jennie age 27 and their children: Earl age 3 and Edwin age 9.[27]

---

[27] 1900 U.S. Federal Census for Chicago, Cook County, Illinois; Supervisors District Number 1, Enumeration District Number 897, Sheets 5A-5B, Lines 48-54

Fig.8. Maria (Keating) Corbett, Photograph Courtesy of Michael T. Tracy © 2010 Michael T. Tracy

Will of Maria Corbett

On Thursday, 22 November 1906 Maria Corbett made out her Last Will and Testament.[28] Later on Thursday, 26 August 1909 she made out a codicil to her will stating that the share of her estate bequeathed to her son, Albert E. Corbett is to be divided equally between him, her granddaughter, Maud S. Corbett and grandson, Albert Corbett.[29] Her son, Thomas Lee Corbett was named executor.

---

[28] Clerk of the Circuit Court of Cook County, Chicago, Illinois
[29] Clerk of the Circuit Court of Cook County, Chicago, Illinois

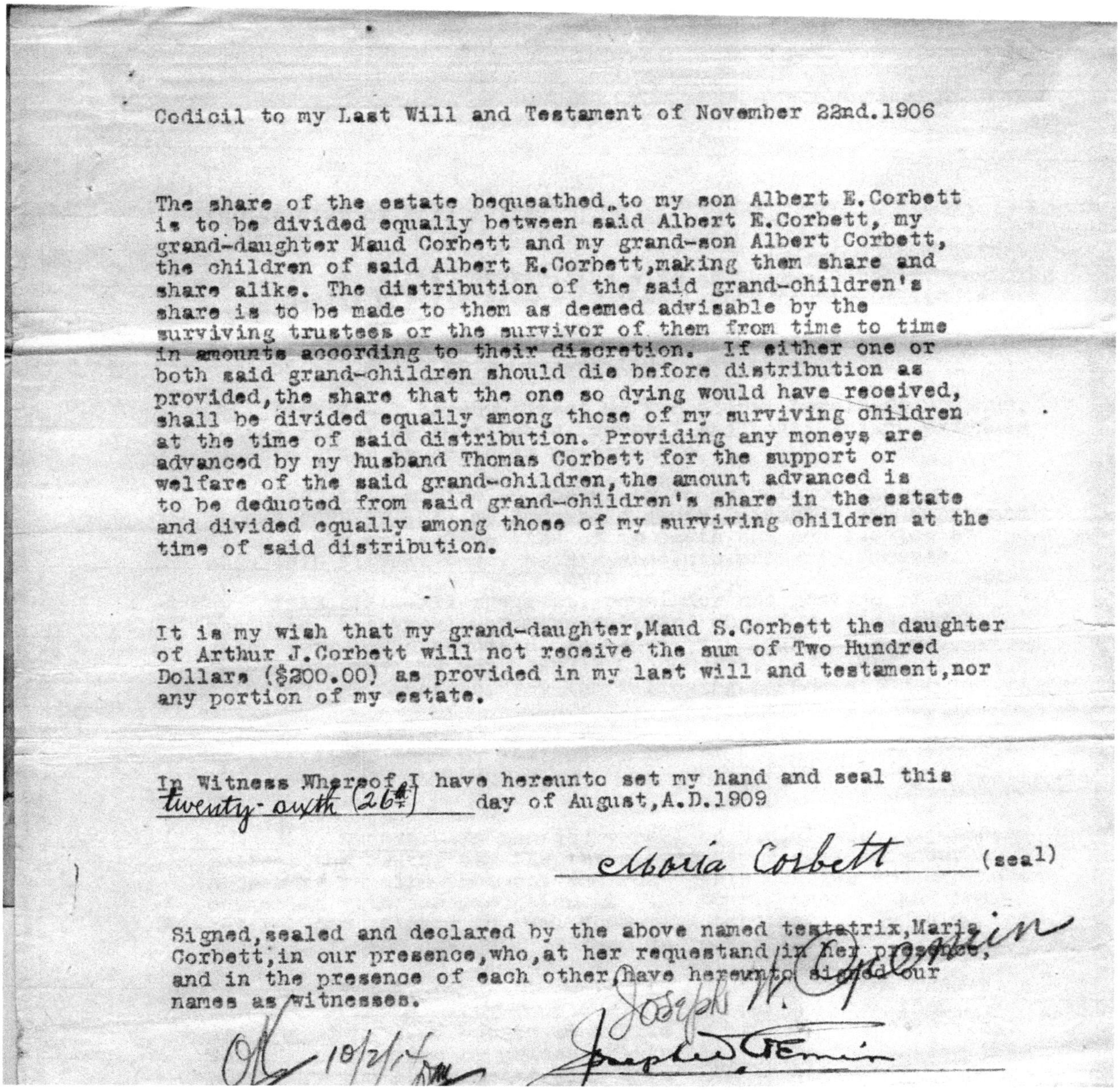

Codicil to my Last Will and Testament of November 22nd, 1906

The share of the estate bequeathed to my son Albert E. Corbett is to be divided equally between said Albert E. Corbett, my grand-daughter Maud Corbett and my grand-son Albert Corbett, the children of said Albert E. Corbett, making them share and share alike. The distribution of the said grand-children's share is to be made to them as deemed advisable by the surviving trustees or the survivor of them from time to time in amounts according to their discretion. If either one or both said grand-children should die before distribution as provided, the share that the one so dying would have received, shall be divided equally among those of my surviving children at the time of said distribution. Providing any moneys are advanced by my husband Thomas Corbett for the support or welfare of the said grand-children, the amount advanced is to be deducted from said grand-children's share in the estate and divided equally among those of my surviving children at the time of said distribution.

It is my wish that my grand-daughter, Maud S. Corbett the daughter of Arthur J. Corbett will not receive the sum of Two Hundred Dollars ($200.00) as provided in my last will and testament, nor any portion of my estate.

In Witness Whereof, I have hereunto set my hand and seal this _twenty-sixth (26th)_ day of August, A.D. 1909

Maria Corbett (seal)

Signed, sealed and declared by the above named testatrix, Maria Corbett, in our presence, who, at her request and in her presence, and in the presence of each other, have hereunto signed our names as witnesses.

Fig.9. Codicil to the Will of Maria Corbett, 26 August 1909

A Golden Wedding

Thomas and Maria Corbett celebrated their 50th Wedding Anniversary on Sunday, 21 November 1909 at their residence in Chicago with their entire family and friends present.[30]

---

[30] *Chicago Daily Newspaper*, 23 November 1909

Fig.10. Chicago Daily Newspaper account of the 50th Wedding Anniversary of Thomas and Maria Corbett, 23 November 1909, Photograph Courtesy of Michael T. Tracy © 2010 Michael T. Tracy

According to the 1910 U.S. Federal Census for Chicago, Cook County, Illinois Thomas is listed as being 73 years of age and working as a carpenter and Maria is 72 years of age with her grandson, Albert age 8.[31] Thomas Corbett died on Friday, 23 August 1912 of liver cancer at the age of 76 at his residence.[32] He was buried on Monday, 26 August 1912 in Mount Olivet Cemetery (Lot 120, Block 25) in Chicago, Illinois.

Death of Maria Corbett

Maria Corbett died on the morning of Thursday, 13 August 1914 at her residence of heart disease at the age of 78.[33]

Fig.11. Maria Corbett Obituary Notice, Chicago Daily Newspaper, 14 August 1914

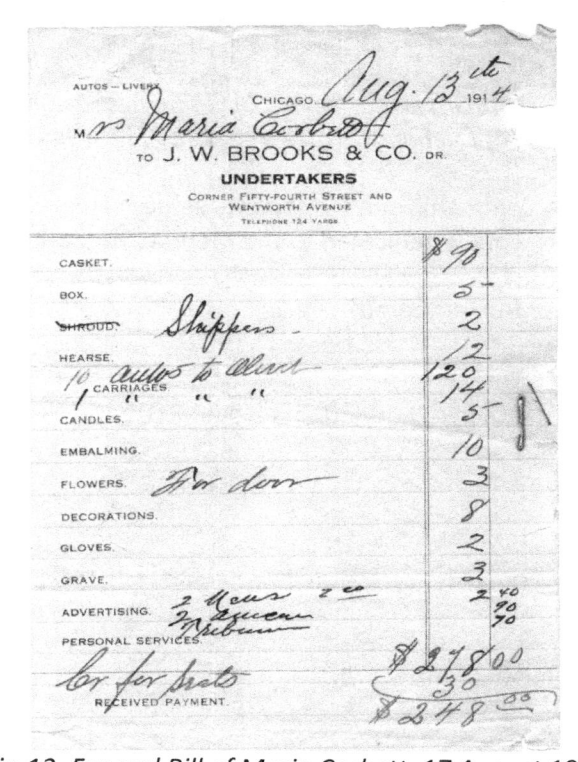

Fig.12. Funeral Bill of Maria Corbett, 17 August 1914

She was buried next to her husband on Monday, 17 August 1914 in Mount Olivet Cemetery (Lot 120, Block 25) in Chicago.

---

[31] 1910 U.S. Federal Census for Chicago, Cook County, Illinois; Supervisors District Number 1, Enumeration District Number 1312, Sheet 7B, Lines 79-81

[32] Death Record of Thomas Corbett, 23 August 1912, Illinois, Cook County Deaths, 1878-1922. Index and Images. Family Search, 2010

[33] Death Record of Maria Corbett, 13 August 1914, Illinois, Cook County Deaths, 1878-1922. Index and Images. Family Search, 2010

Fig.13. Thomas and Maria Corbett Gravesite, Mount Olivet Cemetery, Chicago, Illinois, Photograph Courtesy of Michael T. Tracy © 2010 Michael T. Tracy

Maria Corbett is warmly commemorated in grateful esteem and recognition by her second great grandson, Michael T. Tracy. This work is dedicated to the Memory of Mariah (Maria) (Keating) Corbett.

Memoratus in aeternum (Forever Remembered)

Copyright © 2016 Michael T. Tracy

Catherine (Keating) Kirvan (1840-1929): A Tribute to Her Life and Times
By Her Second Great Grand Nephew, Michael T. Tracy

Catherine Keating was the second daughter born to Patrick Keating and Catherine Ann Walker and most likely was named after her mother. She would marry Patrick Kirvan who was born in Ireland. They had twelve children who were all born in Nichol Township, Wellington County. After her husband's death in 1895 she relocated to Toronto. This then is the narrative of the life and times of Catherine (Keating) Kirvan.

Early years

Catherine Keating was born in 1840 in Pilkington Township, Wellington County, Ontario, Canada. She was the seventh child of Patrick Keating, a farmer, and Catherine Ann Walker. She was listed in the 1851 Canada Census for Pilkington Township, Wellington County as being 9 years of age.[1]

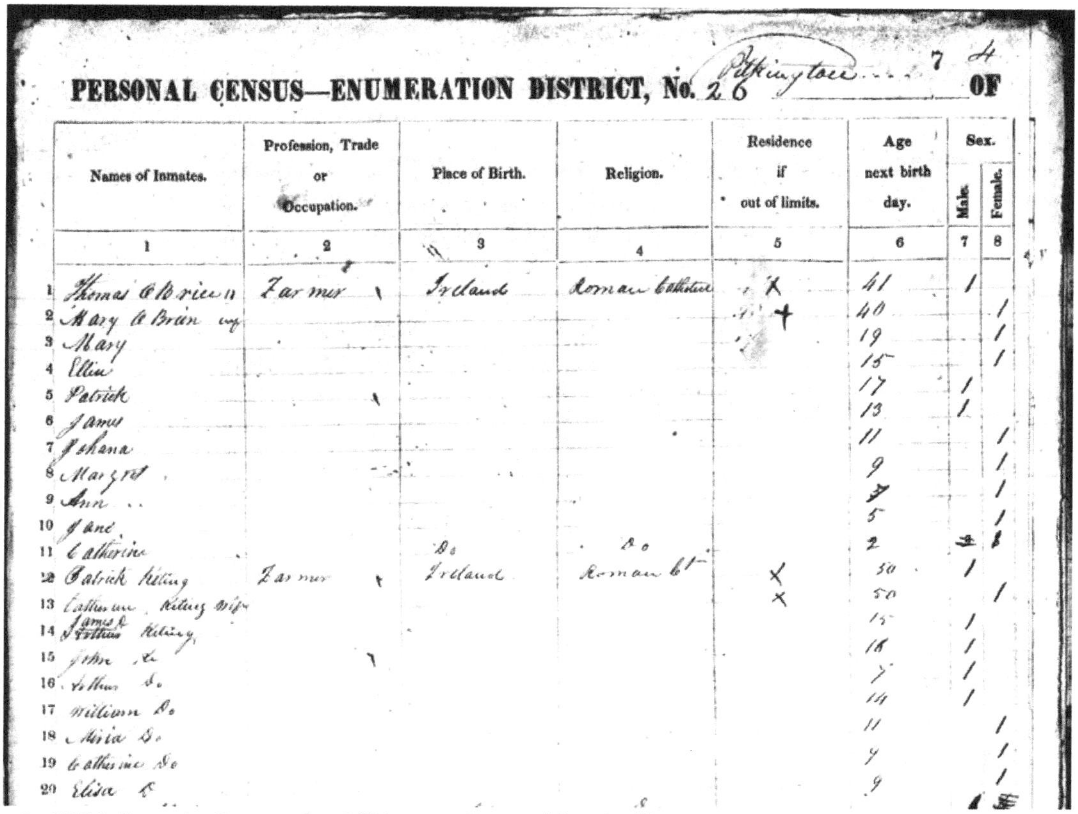
PERSONAL CENSUS—ENUMERATION DISTRICT, No. 26 Pilkington 7 4 OF

	Names of Inmates.	Profession, Trade or Occupation.	Place of Birth.	Religion.	Residence if out of limits.	Age next birth day.	Sex. Male.	Sex. Female.
	1	2	3	4	5	6	7	8
1	Thomas O'Brien	Farmer	Ireland	Roman Catholic	X	41	1	
2	Mary O'Brien wife				+	40		1
3	Mary					19		1
4	Ellen					15		1
5	Patrick					17	1	
6	James					13	1	
7	Johana					11		1
8	Margret					9		1
9	Ann					7		1
10	Jane					5		1
11	Catherine		Do	Do		2		1
12	Patrick Keting	Farmer	Ireland	Roman Ct	X	50	1	
13	Catherine Keting wife				X	50		1
14	James Keting					15	1	
15	John Do					16	1	
16	Arthur Do					7	1	
17	William Do					14	1	
18	Maria Do					11		1
19	Catherine Do					9		1
20	Elisa Do					9		1

Fig.1. 1851 Canada Census for Pilkington Township, Wellington County, Ontario, Canada listing Catherine Keating (Line 19)

Marriage and Family life

Catherine met and later married Patrick Kirvan on Tuesday, 15 December 1863 in Elora officiated by the Reverend John B. Archambault with the witnesses to the marriage being John Powers and Owen

---

[1] 1851 Canada Census for Pilkington Township, Wellington County, Ontario, Canada; Page 7, Line 19

Muldoon. They resided in Nichol Township, Wellington County. Catherine and Patrick had twelve children.

They were:

Mary born on Friday, 23 September 1864[2] and died on Monday, 27 March 1905;[3]
Elizabeth born on Sunday, 1 April 1866[4]
Maurice born on Wednesday, 2 October 1867 and died on Sunday, 28 May 1950;
Patrick born on Tuesday, 16 August 1870;
James born on Friday, 23 June 1871[5] and died on Tuesday, 2 May 1905;[6]
John Joseph born on Saturday, 6 September 1873[7] and died in 1950;
Alice born on Tuesday, 18 January 1876;
Herbert born in 1878;
Catherine Ann born on Wednesday, 20 October 1880[8] and died in 1953;
Ann born in 1881;
Joseph born on Sunday, 13 August 1882[9] and died on Thursday, 26 October 1882;
Frederick born in 1884 and died in 1945.

The family is listed in the 1881 Canada Census for Nichol Township, Wellington County showing Patrick Kirvan as being 37 years of age and working as a laborer and his wife Catherine is 36 years of age with the following children: Mary age 16; Elizabeth age 15; Maurice age 14; Patrick age 11; James age 9; John age 7; Alice age 5; Herbert age 3 and Catherine age 6 months.[10]

According to the 1891 Canada Census for Nichol Township, Wellington County Patrick is listed as being 49 years of age and his wife Catherine is 47 years of age with the following children: Patrick age 21 and working as a cabinet maker; John age 18 and working as a farmer; Alice age 14; Herbert age 12; Ann age 10 and Fred age 7.[11]

---

[2] Baptismal Record of Mary Kirvan, 7 October 1864, Church of Our Lady Records, Guelph, Ontario, Canada

[3] Death Record of Mary McGrogan, 27 March 1905, Ontario, Canada, Deaths, 1869-1938 & Deaths Overseas, 1939-1947. Ancestry.com. Provo, UT, USA: Ancestry.com Operations, Inc., 2010

[4] Baptismal Record of Elizabeth Kirvan, 15 April 1866, Church of Our Lady Records, Guelph, Ontario, Canada

[5] Baptismal Record of James Kirvan, 25 June 1871, Church of Our Lady Records, Guelph, Ontario, Canada

[6] Death Record of James Kirvan, 2 May 1905, Ontario, Canada, Deaths, 1869-1938 & Deaths Overseas, 1939-1947. Ancestry.com. Provo, UT, USA: Ancestry.com Operations, Inc., 2010

[7] Birth Record of John Joseph Kirvan, 6 September 1873, Ontario, Canada, Births, 1869-1913. Ancestry.com. Provo, UT, USA: Ancestry.com Operations, Inc., 2010

[8] Birth Record of Catherine Ann Kirvan, 20 October 1880, Ontario, Canada, Births, 1869-1913. Ancestry.com. Provo, UT, USA: Ancestry.com Operations, Inc., 2010

[9] Birth Record of Joseph Kirvan, 13 August 1882, Ontario, Canada, Births, 1869-1913. Ancestry.com. Provo, UT, USA: Ancestry.com Operations, Inc., 2010

[10] 1881 Canada Census for Nichol Township, Wellington County, Ontario, Canada; Pages 17-18, Lines 24-25; 1-9

[11] 1891 Canada Census for Nichol Township, Wellington County, Ontario, Canada; Page 25, Lines 16-23

Fig.2. 1891 Canada Census for Nichol Township, Wellington County, Ontario, Canada listing Patrick and Catherine Kirvan and Family

Death of Patrick Kirvan

Patrick Kirvan died on Sunday, 22 September 1895 in Nichol Township at the age of 53. He was buried beside his son, Joseph in St. Mary Immaculate Cemetery (Section C) in Elora.

Fig.3. Patrick Kirvan and son Joseph Kirvan Graves, St. Mary Immaculate Cemetery at Elora, Photograph Courtesy of Michael T. Tracy © 2010 Michael T. Tracy

Relocation to Toronto and Death

Catherine's youngest son was residing in Toronto and as Catherine got older she decided to move to Toronto. Catherine resided at 79 First Avenue. She died on Monday, 17 June 1929 at the age of 89.[12]

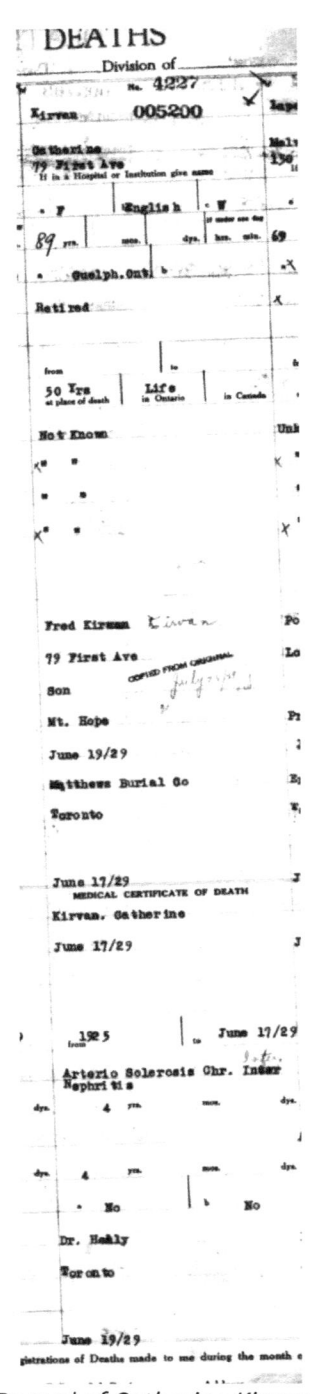

Fig.4. Death Record of Catherine Kirvan, 17 June 1929

---

[12] Death Record of Catherine Kirvan, 17 June 1929, Ontario, Canada, Deaths, 1869-1938 & Deaths Overseas, 1939-1947. Ancestry.com. Provo, UT, USA: Ancestry.com Operations, Inc., 2010

She was buried on Wednesday, 19 June 1929 in Mount Hope Cemetery in Toronto.

Fig.5. Catherine Kirvan Grave, Mount Hope Cemetery, Toronto, Ontario, Canada, Photograph Courtesy of Michael T. Tracy © 2010 Michael T. Tracy

    Catherine (Keating) Kirvan is warmly commemorated in grateful esteem and recognition by her second great grand-nephew, Michael T. Tracy. This work is dedicated to the Memory of Catherine (Keating) Kirvan.

Memoratus in aeternum (Forever Remembered)

Copyright © 2016 Michael T. Tracy

William Keating (1845-1921): A Tribute to His Life and Times
By His Second Great Grand Nephew, Michael T. Tracy

William Keating was a farmer and life-long resident of Pilkington Township, Wellington County. He married Mary McQuinn of Nichol Township and they had thirteen children who were all born in Pilkington Township. Keating, like his father before him and some of his brothers, was a prominent farmer. This then is the narrative of the life and times of William Keating.

Early years

William Keating was born on Thursday, 2 October 1845 in Pilkington Township, Wellington County, Ontario, Canada.[1] He was the eighth child of Patrick Keating, a farmer, and Catherine Ann Walker. He was listed in the 1851 Canada Census for Pilkington Township as being 14 [sic] years of age.[2]

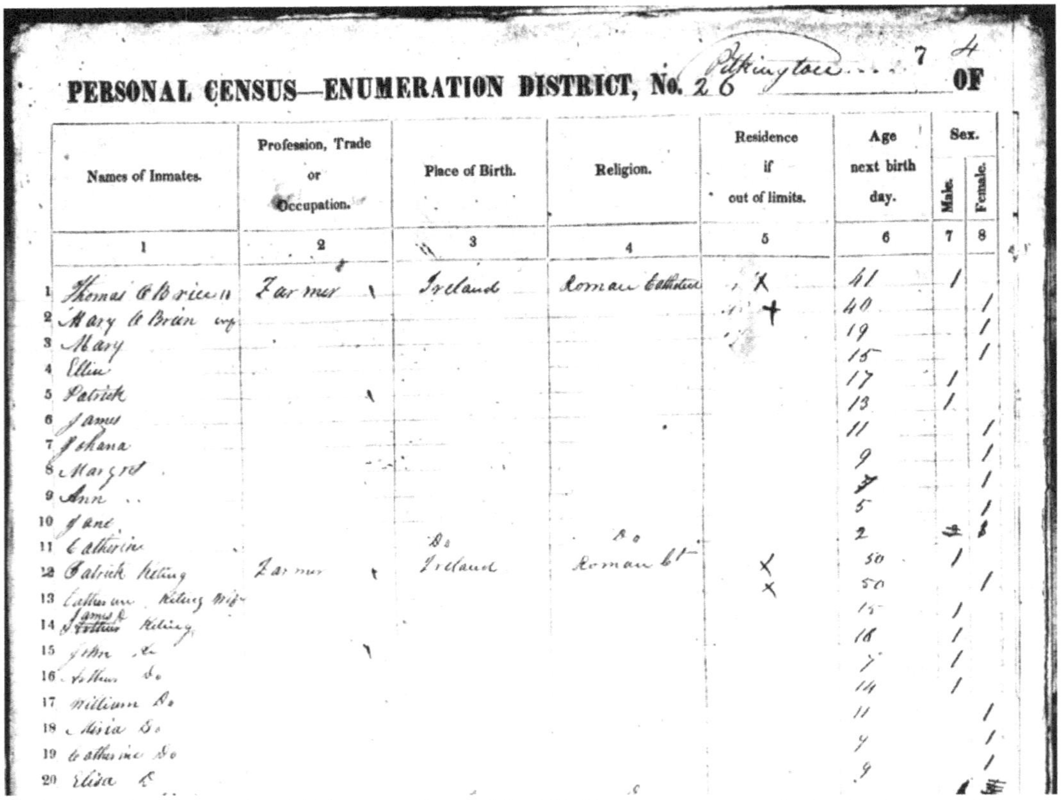
PERSONAL CENSUS—ENUMERATION DISTRICT, No. 26 Pilkington 7 4 OF

	Names of Inmates.	Profession, Trade or Occupation.	Place of Birth.	Religion.	Residence if out of limits.	Age next birth day.	Sex. Male.	Sex. Female.
	1	2	3	4	5	6	7	8
1	Thomas O'Brien	Farmer	Ireland	Roman Catholic	X	41	1	
2	Mary O'Brien wife				+	40		1
3	Mary					19		1
4	Ellen					15		1
5	Patrick					17	1	
6	James					13	1	
7	Johana					11		1
8	Margret					9		1
9	Ann					7		1
10	Jane					5		1
11	Catherine		Do	Do		2		1
12	Patrick Keting	Farmer	Ireland	Roman Ct	X	50	1	
13	Catherine Keting wife				X	50		1
14	James Keting					15	1	
15	John Do					18	1	
16	Arthur Do					7	1	
17	William Do					14	1	
18	Maria Do					11		1
19	Catharine Do					9		1
20	Eliza Do					9		1

Fig.1. 1851 Canada Census for Pilkington Township, Wellington County, Ontario, Canada listing William Keating (Line 17)

[1] Death Record of William Keating, 19 January 1921, Ontario, Canada, Deaths, 1869-1938 & Deaths Overseas, 1939-1947. Ancestry.com. Provo, UT, USA: Ancestry.com Operations, Inc., 2010

[2] 1851 Canada Census for Pilkington Township, Wellington County, Ontario, Canada; Page 7, Line 17

Marriage and Family life

Keating purchased his farmland located at Lot 14, Concession 1 before his marriage.

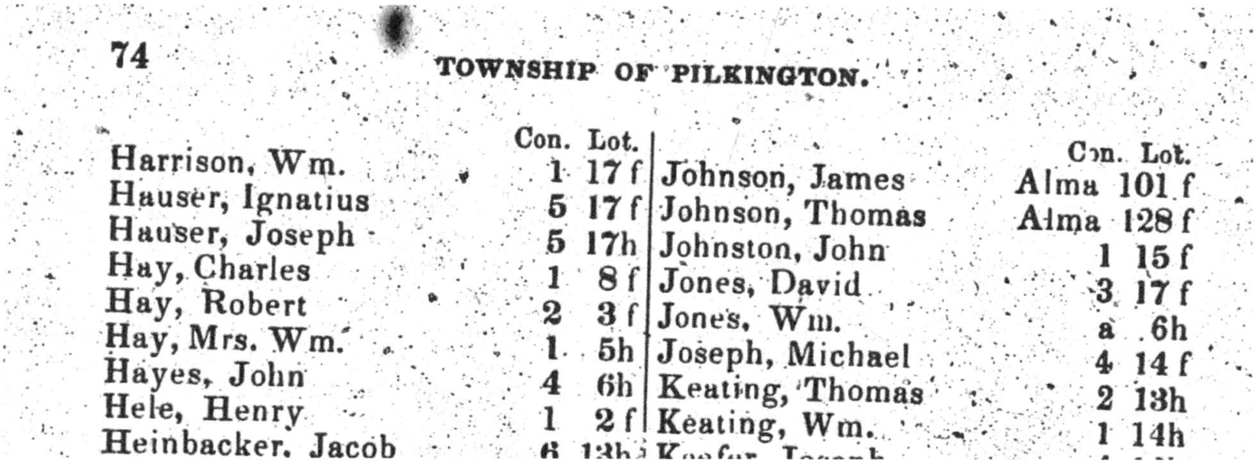

74 TOWNSHIP OF PILKINGTON.

	Con.	Lot.		Con.	Lot.
Harrison, Wm.	1	17 f	Johnson, James	Alma	101 f
Hauser, Ignatius	5	17 f	Johnson, Thomas	Alma	128 f
Hauser, Joseph	5	17h	Johnston, John	1	15 f
Hay, Charles	1	8 f	Jones, David	3	17 f
Hay, Robert	2	3 f	Jones, Wm.	a	6h
Hay, Mrs. Wm.	1	5h	Joseph, Michael	4	14 f
Hayes, John	4	6h	Keating, Thomas	2	13h
Hele, Henry	1	2 f	Keating, Wm.	1	14h
Heinbacker, Jacob	6	13h	[illegible]		

Fig.2. 1867 Farmers and Business Directory for the County of Wellington listing William Keating

He met and later was married to Mary McQuinn of Nichol Township on Tuesday, 26 November 1867 in Pilkington by the Reverend John B. Archambault with the witnesses to the marriage being Peter Daly and William's sister, Elizabeth Keating. They had thirteen children who were all born in Pilkington Township. They were:

Catherine born on Monday, 23 November 1868[3]
Elizabeth J., born on Wednesday, 1 June 1870;[4]
Maria Josephine born on Friday, 29 December 1871[5] and died on Thursday, 15 September 1927;[6]
John Patrick born on Tuesday, 2 September 1873;[7]
Mary Agnes born on Wednesday, 10 May 1876[8] and died in June of 1950;
Rose Ellen born on Saturday, 6 July 1878[9] and died on Friday, 19 July 1957;
Felix born on Sunday, 29 February 1880[10] and died in 1959;
Bridget born on Sunday, 17 April 1881[11] and died on Tuesday, 25 March 1952;
Arthur born on Friday, 3 August 1883[12] and died in 1951;
William Francis born on Thursday, 11 December 1884;[13]

---

3 Baptismal Record of Catherine Keating, 8 December 1868, Church of Our Lady Records, Guelph, Ontario, Canada
4 Baptismal Record of Elizabeth Keating, 26 June 1870, Church of Our Lady Records, Guelph, Ontario, Canada
5 Baptismal Record of Maria Josephine Keating, 21 January 1872, Church of Our Lady Records, Guelph, Ontario, Canada
6 Death Record of Maria J. Keating, 15 September 1927, Ontario, Canada, Deaths, 1869-1938 & Deaths Overseas, 1939-1947. Ancestry.com. Provo, UT, USA: Ancestry.com Operations, Inc., 2010
7 Baptismal Record of John Patrick Keating, 26 September 1873, Church of Our Lady Records, Guelph, Ontario, Canada
8 Baptismal Record of Mary Agnes Keating, 4 June 1876, Church of Our Lady Records, Guelph, Ontario, Canada
9 Baptismal Record of Rose Ellen Keating, 24 July 1878, Church of Our Lady Records, Guelph, Ontario, Canada
10 Baptismal Record of Felix Keating, 16 March 1880, Church of Our Lady Records, Guelph, Ontario, Canada
11 Baptismal Record of Bridget Keating, 10 May 1881, Church of Our Lady Records, Guelph, Ontario, Canada
12 Baptismal Record of Arthur Keating, 19 August 1883, Church of Our Lady Records, Guelph, Ontario, Canada
13 Baptismal Record of William Francis Keating, 13 December 1884, Church of Our Lady Records, Guelph, Ontario, Canada

Thomas Joseph born on Tuesday, 21 September 1886[14] and died in 1979;
Regina Gertrude born on Wednesday, 12 September 1888[15] and died on Tuesday, 18 January 1898;[16]
Margaret born on Thursday, 25 September 1890[17] and died on Wednesday, 7 March 1928.[18]

The family is listed in the 1871 Canada Census for Pilkington Township showing William Keating as being 26 years of age and working as a farmer and his wife Mary is 24 years of age with the following children: Catherine age 2 and Elizabeth age 10 months.[19]

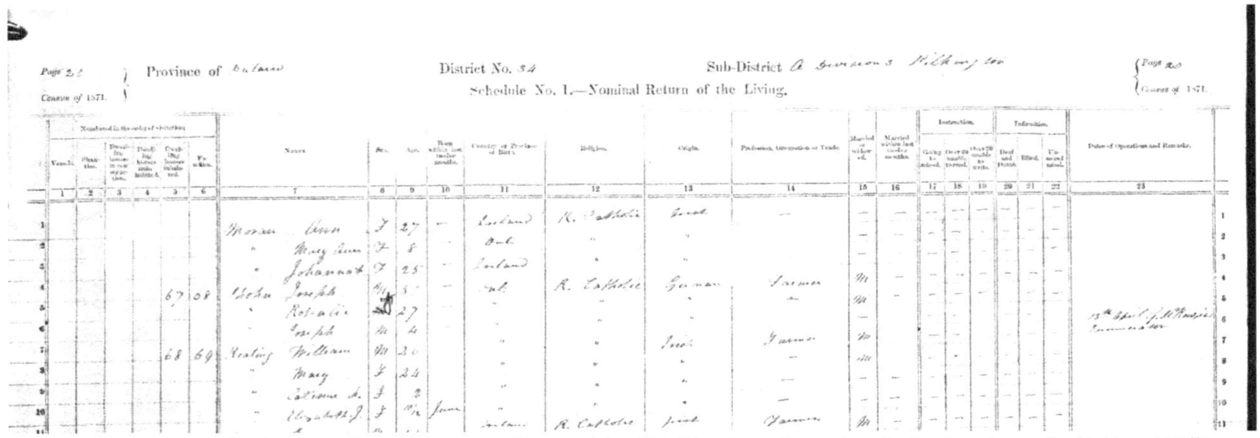

Fig.3. 1871 Canada Census for Pilkington Township, Wellington County, Ontario, Canada listing William Keating and Family

According to the 1881 Canada Census for Pilkington Township William is listed as being 36 years of age and working as a farmer and his wife Mary is 32 years of age with the following children: John age 7; Mary age 5; Rose age 3 and Felix age 1.[20]

---

[14] Baptismal Record of Thomas Joseph Keating, 3 October 1886, Church of Our Lady Records, Guelph, Ontario, Canada

[15] Baptismal Record of Regina Gertrude Keating, 14 October 1888, Church of Our Lady Records, Guelph, Ontario, Canada

[16] Death Record of Regina Gertrude Keating, 18 January 1898, Ontario, Canada, Deaths, 1869-1938 & Deaths Overseas, 1939-1947. Ancestry.com. Provo, UT, USA: Ancestry.com Operations, Inc., 2010

[17] Baptismal Record of Margaret Keating, 9 October 1890, Church of Our Lady Records, Guelph, Ontario, Canada

[18] Death Record of Margaret Hawkins, 7 March 1928, Illinois, Deaths & Stillbirths Index, 1916-1947. Ancestry.com. Provo, UT, USA: Ancestry.com Operations, Inc., 2011

[19] 1871 Canada Census for Pilkington Township, Wellington County, Ontario, Canada; Page 20, Lines 7-10

[20] 1881 Canada Census for Pilkington Township, Wellington County, Ontario, Canada; Page 2, Lines 15-20

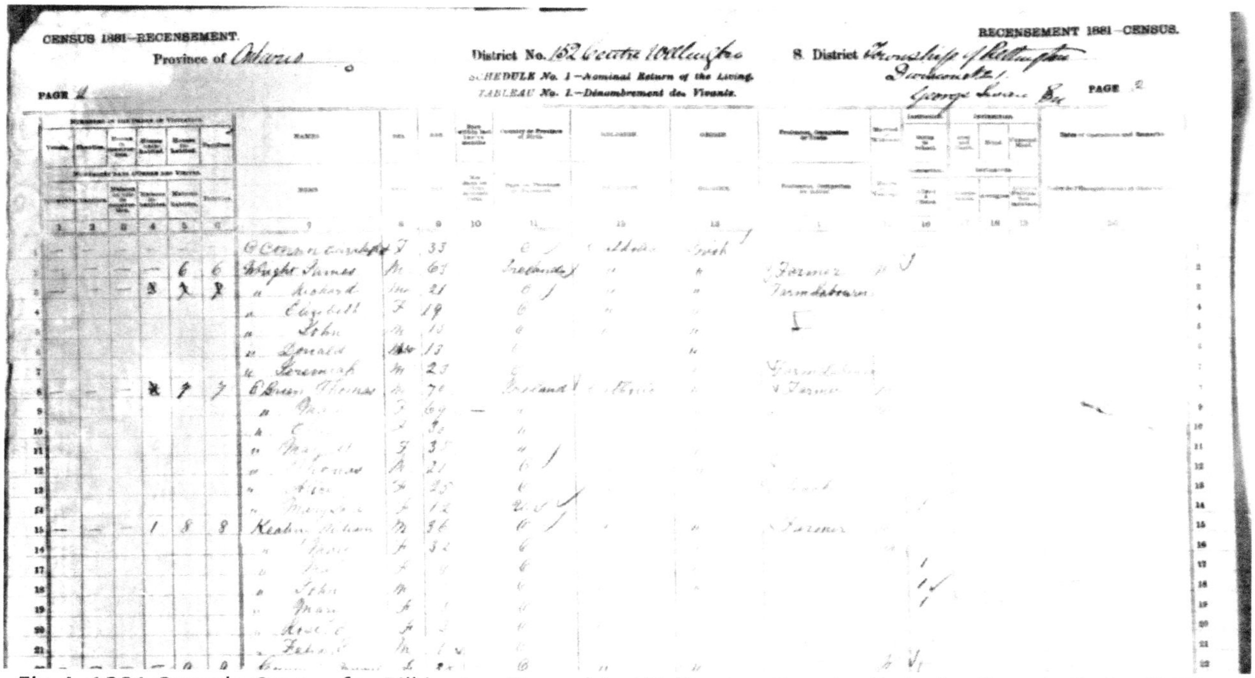

Fig.4. 1881 Canada Census for Pilkington Township, Wellington County, Ontario, Canada listing William Keating and Family

The family is listed in the 1891 Canada Census for Pilkington Township showing William being 46 years of age and working as a farmer and his wife Mary is 44 years of age with the following children: Mariah age 19; John age 17 and working as a farmer; Mary age 14; Rose Ellen age 12; Felix age 11; Bridget age 10; Arthur age 9; William age 7; Thomas age 5; Regina age 3 and Margaret age 6 months.[21]

---

[21] 1891 Canada Census for Pilkington Township, Wellington County, Ontario, Canada; Page 15, Lines 12-24

Fig.5. 1891 Canada Census for Pilkington Township, Wellington County, Ontario, Canada listing William Keating and Family

By 1901 the Keating family is listed in the Census for Pilkington Township with William being 59 years of age and working as a farmer and his wife Mary is 53 years of age with the following children: Maria age 29; John age 27 and working as a farmer; Felix age 21 and working as a farm laborer; Bridget age 19; Arthur age 17 and William age 16.[22]

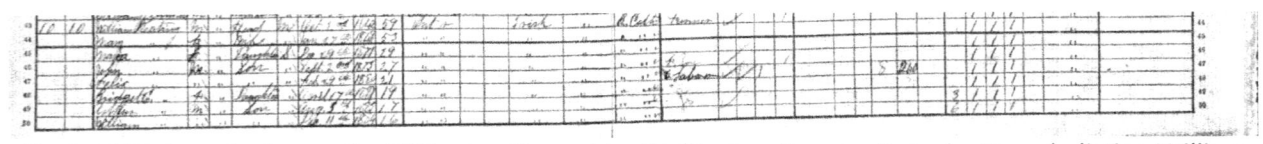

Fig.6. 1901 Canada Census for Pilkington Township, Wellington County, Ontario, Canada listing William Keating and Family

In the 1911 Canada Census for Pilkington Township William is 68 years of age and working as a farmer and his wife Mary is 64 years of age with the following children: Maria age 39; Bridget age 30 and Arthur age 28 and working as a farmer.[23]

---

[22] 1901 Canada Census for Pilkington Township, Wellington County, Ontario, Canada; Page 1, Lines 43-50
[23] 1911 Canada Census for Pilkington Township, Wellington County, Ontario, Canada; Page 8, Lines 46-50

Death of William Keating

William Keating died on Wednesday, 19 January 1921 at his residence of indigestion at the age of 75.[24]

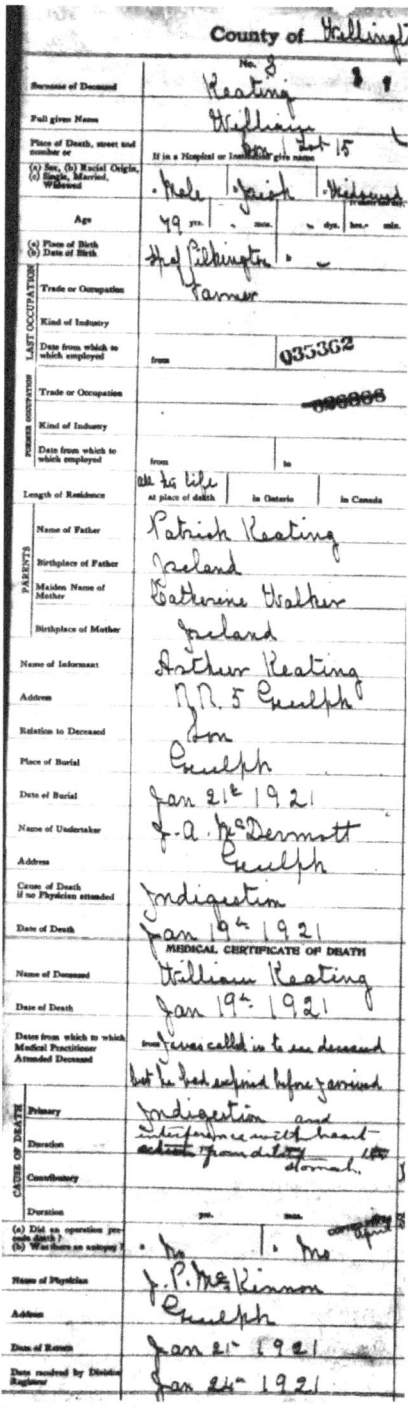

Fig.7. Death Record of William Keating, 19 January 1921

---

[24] Death Record of William Keating, 19 January 1921, Ontario, Canada, Deaths, 1869-1938 & Deaths Overseas, 1939-1947. Ancestry.com. Provo, UT, USA: Ancestry.com Operations, Inc., 2010

His obituary notice was published in the *Guelph Mercury & Advertiser Newspaper* of Thursday, 20 January 1921:

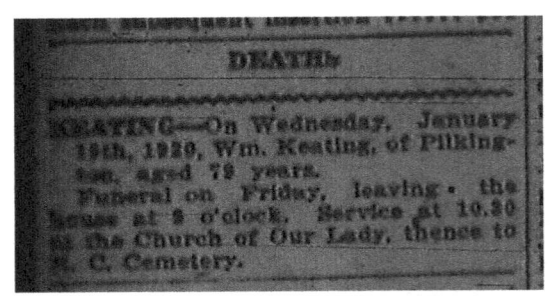

Fig.8. William Keating Obituary, Guelph Mercury & Advertiser Newspaper, 20 January 1921

He was buried in the Keating family burial lot in St. Joseph's Catholic Cemetery (Section E-149) on Friday, 21 January 1921 in Guelph.

Fig.9. William Keating and Family Graves, St. Joseph's Catholic Cemetery, Guelph, Ontario, Canada, Photograph Courtesy of Michael T. Tracy © 2010 Michael T. Tracy

Mary Keating, his wife, died nine years previously on Saturday, 14 December 1912 at the age of 64.[25]

---

[25] Death Record of Mary Keating, 14 December 1912, Ontario, Canada, Deaths, 1869-1938 & Deaths Overseas, 1939-1947. Ancestry.com. Provo, UT, USA: Ancestry.com Operations, Inc., 2010

Fig.10. Death Record of Mary Keating, 14 December 1912

She was buried in St. Joseph's Catholic Cemetery (Section E-149) on Monday, 16 December 1912. Their gravestone reads: "Mary, wife of William Keating, died December 14, 1912, aged 65 [sic] years. William Keating died January 19, 1921, in his 79th [sic] year. May their souls rest in peace. Additionally on the left side: Keating Maria Josephine died September 15, 1927 aged 56 years. Bridget E. Keating died March 25, 1952 aged 71 years."

William Keating is warmly commemorated in grateful esteem and recognition by his second great grand-nephew, Michael T. Tracy. This work is dedicated to the Memory of William Keating.

Memoratus in aeternum (Forever Remembered)

Copyright © 2016 Michael T. Tracy

Elizabeth (Keating) Crow (1850-1906): A Tribute to Her Life and Times
By Her Second Great Grand Nephew, Michael T. Tracy

Elizabeth Keating was the last child of Patrick and Catherine Ann Keating. She grew up in Pilkington Township, Wellington County, Ontario, Canada and later worked for her sister Maria Corbett and husband Thomas Corbett as a servant in their hotel in Fergus. Elizabeth would meet and marry an Englishman named Samuel Gilbert Crow and they would move to Arthur where they had their first three children. By 1882 the family relocated to Toronto where they had two additional children. Elizabeth and Samuel resided in Toronto for the rest of their lives. This then is the narrative of the life and times of Elizabeth (Keating) Crow.

Early years

There is some discrepancy as to when exactly Elizabeth Keating was born. She was most likely born on Saturday, 28 September 1850 in Pilkington Township, Wellington County. She was the ninth child of Patrick Keating, a farmer, and Catherine Ann Walker. Elizabeth is listed in the 1851 Canada Census for Pilkington Township, Wellington County as being 9 [sic] years of age.[1]

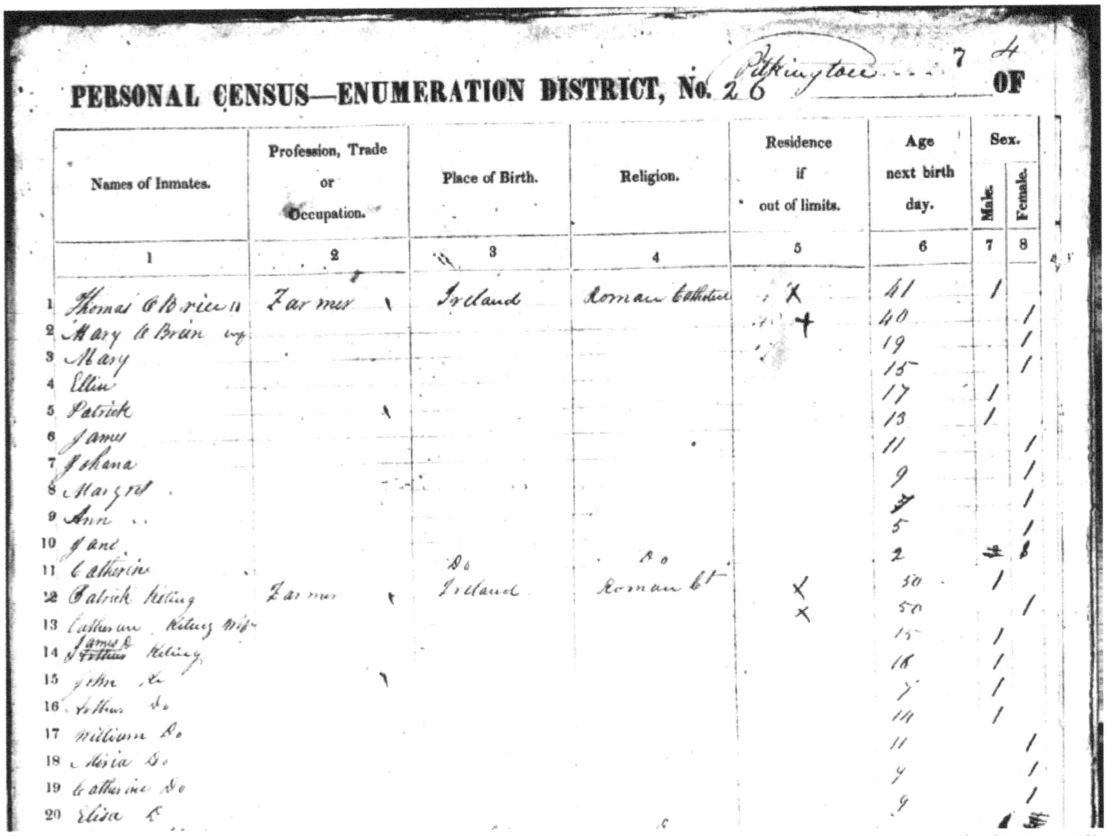

PERSONAL CENSUS—ENUMERATION DISTRICT, No. 26 Pilkington 7 4 OF

	Names of Inmates.	Profession, Trade or Occupation.	Place of Birth.	Religion.	Residence if out of limits.	Age next birth day.	Sex. Male.	Sex. Female.
	1	2	3	4	5	6	7	8
1	Thomas O'Brien	Farmer	Ireland	Roman Catholic	X	41	/	
2	Mary O'Brien wife				+	40		/
3	Mary					19		/
4	Ellin					15		/
5	Patrick					17	/	
6	James					13	/	
7	Johana					11		/
8	Margret					9		/
9	Ann					7		/
10	Jane					5		/
11	Catherine		Do	Do		2		/
12	Patrick Keating	Farmer	Ireland	Roman Ct	X	50	/	
13	Catherine Keating wife				X	50		/
14	James Keating					15	/	
15	John Do					18	/	
16	Arthur Do					7	/	
17	William Do					14	/	
18	Maria Do					11		/
19	Catherine Do					4		/
20	Eliza Do					9		/

Fig.1. 1851 Canada Census for Pilkington Township, Wellington County, Ontario, Canada listing Elizabeth Keating (Line 20)

[1] 1851 Canada Census for Pilkington Township, Wellington County, Ontario, Canada; Page 7, Line 19

By 1871 she is listed in the Canada Census for Fergus, Wellington County, Ontario, Canada as being 21 years of age and working as a servant in the hotel of her sister Maria (Keating) and Thomas Corbett.[2]

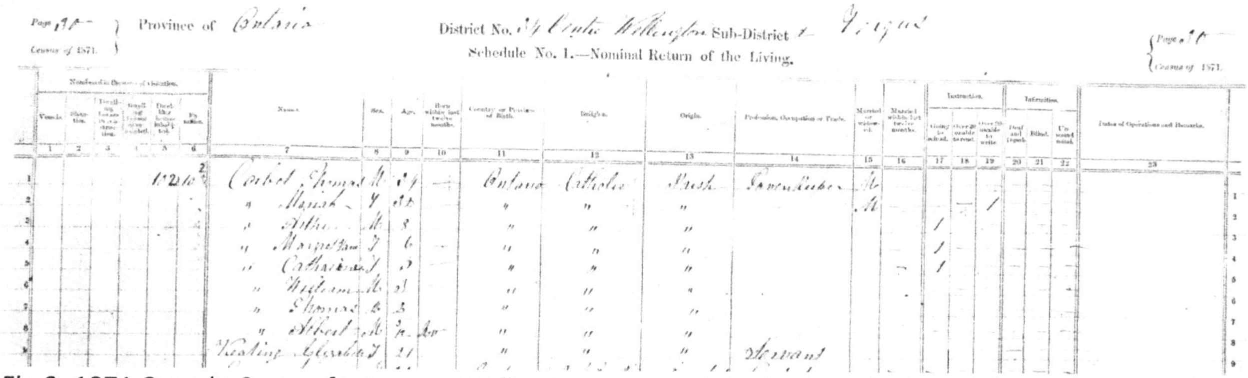

Province of Ontario — District No. 34 Centre Wellington Sub-District 2 Fergus

Schedule No. 1.—Nominal Return of the Living.

Line	Name	Sex	Age	Country or Province of Birth	Religion	Origin	Profession, Occupation or Trade	Married or widowed
1	Corbet, Thomas	M	39	Ontario	Catholic	Irish	Innkeeper	M
2	" Mariah	F	32	"	"	"		M
3	" Arthur	M	8	"	"	"		
4	" Margaret Ann	F	6	"	"	"		
5	" Catharine	F	3	"	"	"		
6	" William	M	3	"	"	"		
7	" Thomas	M	2	"	"	"		
8	" Albert	M	2/12 Nov	"	"	"		
9	Keating, Elizabeth	F	21	"	"	"	Servant	

Fig.2. 1871 Canada Census for Fergus, Wellington County, Ontario, Canada listing Elizabeth Keating (Line 9)

Marriage and Family life

Elizabeth Keating met and later married Samuel Gilbert Crow on Wednesday, 16 April 1873 in St. Catharines in what today is known as Niagara County, Ontario, Canada.[3]

---

2 1871 Canada Census for Fergus, Wellington County, Ontario, Canada; Page 30, Line 9

3 Marriage Record of Elizabeth Keating, 16 April 1873, Ontario, Canada, Marriages, 1801-1928. Ancestry.com & Genealogical Research Library. Provo, UT, USA: Ancestry.com Operations, Inc., 2010

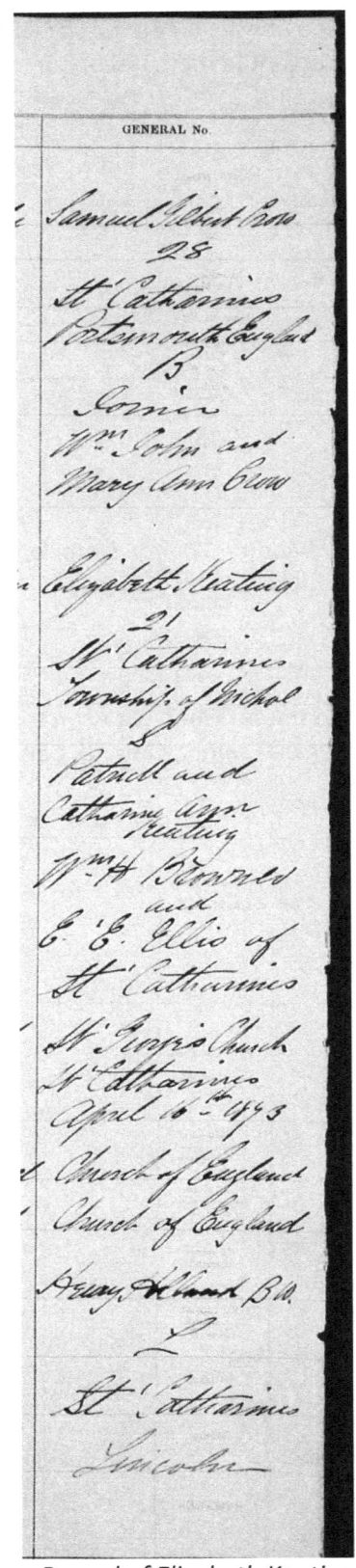

GENERAL No.
Samuel Gilbert Crow
28
St Catharines
Portsmouth England
B
Joiner
Wm John and
Mary Ann Crow
Elizabeth Keating
21
St Catharines
Township of Nichol
S
Patrick and
Catharine Ann
Keating
Wm H Bowyer
and
C. E. Ellis of
St Catharines
St George's Church
St Catharines
April 16th 1873
Church of England
Church of England
Henry Holland B.A.
St Catharines
Lincoln

Fig.3. Marriage Record of Elizabeth Keating, 16 April 1873

After their marriage the couple resided in Arthur. They had five children. They were:

Mary Ann born on Monday, 22 June 1874 and died on Monday, 22 October 1951;
Matilda Mabel born on Monday, 28 February 1876[4] and died on Sunday, 30 September 1877;[5]
Sarah Lavinia born on Thursday, 28 August 1879[6] and died on Saturday, 29 August 1964;
William John born on Thursday, 11 January 1883[7] and died on Friday, 29 January 1943;
Elizabeth Drucellia born on Wednesday, 28 January 1885[8] and died in 1950.

Relocation to Toronto

After residing in Arthur, Wellington County, the Crow family relocated to Toronto sometime in 1882. Samuel Crow is listed in the 1883 *Toronto City Directory* as working as a carpenter for the W & J.G. Greey Company and residing at 109 Queen Street.

Fig.4. 1883 Toronto City Directory listing Samuel Crow

---

[4] Birth Record of Matilda Mabel Crow, 28 February 1876, Ontario, Canada, Births, 1869-1913. Ancestry.com. Provo, UT, USA: Ancestry.com Operations, Inc., 2010

[5] Death Record of Matilda Mabel Crow, 30 September 1877, Ontario, Canada, Deaths, 1869-1938 & Deaths Overseas, 1939-1947. Ancestry.com. Provo, UT, USA: Ancestry.com Operations, Inc., 2010

[6] Birth Record of Sarah Lavinia Crow, 28 August 1879, Ontario, Canada, Births, 1869-1913. Ancestry.com. Provo, UT, USA: Ancestry.com Operations, Inc., 2010

[7] Birth Record of William John Crow, 11 January 1883, Ontario, Canada, Births, 1869-1913. Ancestry.com. Provo, UT, USA: Ancestry.com Operations, Inc., 2010

[8] Birth Record of Elizabeth Drucellia Crown, 28 January 1885, Ontario, Canada, Births, 1869-1913. Ancestry.com. Provo, UT, USA: Ancestry.com Operations, Inc., 2010

According to the 1901 Canada Census for Toronto, Ontario Samuel Crow is listed as being 55 years of age and working as a dress cutter and his wife Elizabeth is 49 years of age with the following children: Mary age 25 and working as a dress maker; Lavinia age 20 and working as a milliner; William age 18 and Elizabeth age 16.[9]

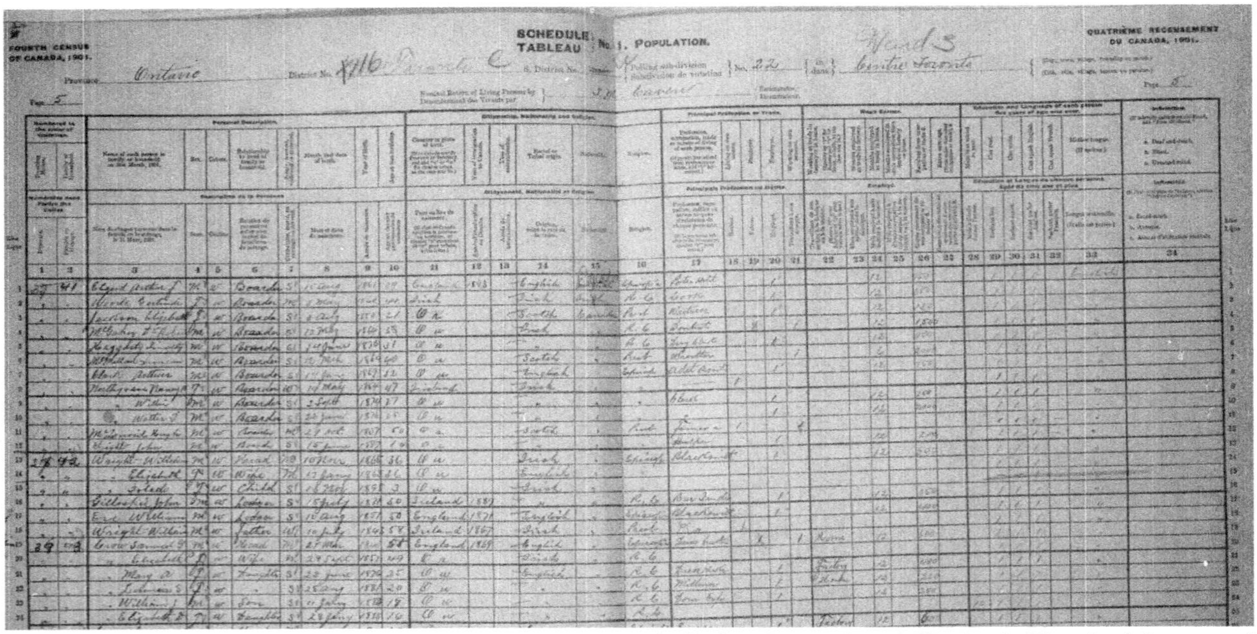

Fig.5. 1901 Canada Census for Toronto, Ontario, Canada listing Samuel and Elizabeth (Keating) Crow and Family

By 1903 the family had moved to 3 Henry Street and Samuel was working as a dress cutter, Elizabeth was a dress maker and their daughter Mary was also a dress maker.[10] Two years later the family had moved again to 270 Avenue Road.[11]

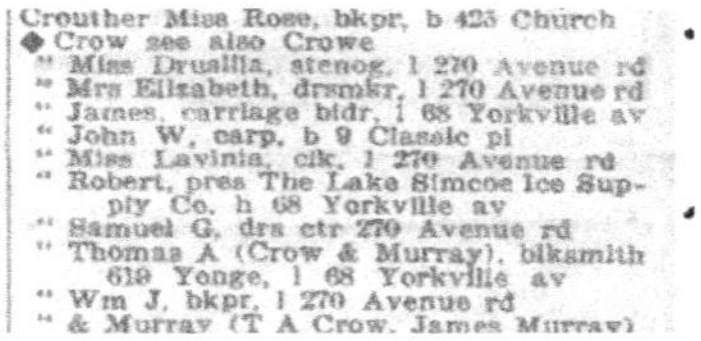

Crouther Miss Rose, bkpr, b 425 Church
◆ Crow see also Crowe
" Miss Drusilla, stenog, l 270 Avenue rd
" Mrs Elizabeth, drsmkr, l 270 Avenue rd
" James, carriage bldr, l 68 Yorkville av
" John W, carp, b 9 Classic pl
" Miss Lavinia, clk, l 270 Avenue rd
" Robert, pres The Lake Simcoe Ice Supply Co, h 68 Yorkville av
" Samuel G, drs ctr 270 Avenue rd
" Thomas A (Crow & Murray), blksmith 619 Yonge, l 68 Yorkville av
" Wm J, bkpr, l 270 Avenue rd
" & Murray (T A Crow, James Murray)

Fig.6. 1905 Toronto City Directory listing the Crow Family

---

[9] 1901 Canada Census for Toronto, Ontario, Canada; Page 5, Lines 19-24

[10] 1903 *Toronto City Directory* p. 395

[11] 1905 *Toronto City Directory* p. 420

Death of Elizabeth Crow

Elizabeth (Keating) Crow died on Thursday, 25 October 1906 at the age of 56 in Toronto.[12] She was buried on Saturday, 27 October 1906 in Mount Hope Cemetery in Toronto.

Death of Samuel Crow

Samuel Crow died on Tuesday, 16 April 1907 at the age of 61 in Toronto.[13] He was buried next to his wife in Mount Hope Cemetery on Thursday, 18 April 1907 in Toronto.

Fig.7. Graves of Elizabeth and Samuel Crow and Family, Mount Hope Cemetery, Toronto, Ontario, Canada, Photograph Courtesy of Michael T. Tracy © 2010 Michael T. Tracy

---

[12] Death Record of Elizabeth Crow, 25 October 1906, Ontario, Canada, Deaths, 1869-1938 & Deaths Overseas, 1939-1947. Ancestry.com. Provo, UT, USA: Ancestry.com Operations, Inc., 2010

[13] Death Record of Samuel G. Crow, 16 April 1907, Ontario, Canada, Deaths, 1869-1938 & Deaths Overseas, 1939-1947. Ancestry.com. Provo, UT, USA: Ancestry.com Operations, Inc., 2010

Elizabeth (Keating) Crow is warmly commemorated in grateful esteem and recognition by her second great grand-nephew, Michael T. Tracy. This work is dedicated to the Memory of Elizabeth (Keating) Crow.

Memoratus in aeternum (Forever Remembered)

Copyright © 2016 Michael T. Tracy

Thomas Keating (1804-1882): A Tribute to his Life and Times
By His Third Great Grand Nephew, Michael T. Tracy

Thomas Keating was the younger brother of Patrick Keating and was the first known member of the family to emigrate from Ireland to Canada. He resided in Guelph, Wellington County. His brother Patrick and his family resided with him in Guelph in 1837-38 before relocating to Pilkington Township. Thomas was the Postmaster of Guelph and later became the Register of the Surrogate Court also of Guelph. Thomas would marry Mary Ann Richardson and have five children who were all born in Guelph. This then is the narrative of the life and times of Thomas Keating.

Early years

Thomas Keating was born in about 1804 in Eglish Parish, Kings County, Ireland.[1] Very little is known of his youth while in Ireland. Keating left at a young age and immigrated to Canada settling in Guelph, Wellington County by 1830. He was the first known member of the Keating family to settle in Canada. According to Mr. John Keleher, who wrote an article in the Guelph Historical Society's annual publication, "Historic Guelph," stated that: "Thomas Keating kept the Post Office in the stone store on Lot 1 built for J.D. Oliver next to the hotel which Keating and his brother Patrick occupied on Lot 2." Thomas Keating was Postmaster of Guelph in 1830-32.

Marriage and Family life

Thomas Keating met and later married Mary Ann Richardson sometime before 1837. They had five children who were all born in Guelph. They were:

Thomas Auchmuty born on Monday, 30 October 1837 and died on Sunday, 12 March 1892;[2]
Jemima Mary born on Friday, 1 May 1840 and died on Tuesday, 30 May 1916;[3]
Jane born on Tuesday, 17 February 1846 and died on Monday, 31 December 1928;[4]
Anna Maria born on Wednesday, 17 May 1848 and died on Tuesday, 29 April 1930;[5]
John Howitt born in 1851.

---

[1] Death Record of Thomas Keating, 12 May 1882, Ontario, Canada, Deaths, 1869-1938 & Deaths Overseas, 1939-1947. Ancestry.com. Provo, UT, USA: Ancestry.com Operations, Inc., 2010

[2] Death Record of Thomas A. Keating, 12 March 1892, Ontario, Canada, Deaths, 1869-1938 & Deaths Overseas, 1939-1947. Ancestry.com. Provo, UT, USA: Ancestry.com Operations, Inc., 2010

[3] Death Record of Jemima M. Lamprey, 30 May 1916, Ontario, Canada, Deaths, 1869-1938 & Deaths Overseas, 1939-1947. Ancestry.com. Provo, UT, USA: Ancestry.com Operations, Inc., 2010

[4] Death Record of Jane Keating, 31 December 1928, Ontario, Canada, Deaths, 1869-1938 & Deaths Overseas, 1939-1947. Ancestry.com. Provo, UT, USA: Ancestry.com Operations, Inc., 2010

[5] Death Record of Anna M. Keating, 29 April 1930, Ontario, Canada, Deaths, 1869-1938 & Deaths Overseas, 1939-1947. Ancestry.com. Provo, UT, USA: Ancestry.com Operations, Inc., 2010

The family is listed in the 1861 Canada Census for Guelph, Wellington County showing Thomas Keating as being 55 years of age and working as a Register of the Surrogate Court and his wife Mary Ann is 50 years of age with the following children: Mary age 19; Jane age 16; Maria Ann age 14 and John age 10.[6]

Fig.1. 1861 Canada Census for Guelph, Wellington County, Ontario, Canada listing Thomas Keating and Family

According to the 1871 Canada Census for Guelph, Wellington County Thomas is listed as being 65 years of age and working as a Register of the Surrogate Court and residing with the following children: Jemima age 26 [sic]; Jeannie age 23 [sic] and Annie age 21 [sic].[7]

Fig.2. 1871 Canada Census for Guelph, Wellington County, Ontario, Canada listing Thomas Keating and Family

---

[6] 1861 Canada Census for Guelph, Wellington County, Ontario, Canada; Page 39, Lines 42-47
[7] 1871 Canada Census for Guelph, Wellington County, Ontario, Canada; Page 64, Lines 6-9

Death of Mary Ann Keating

Mary Ann Keating died on Monday, 20 February 1871 at the age of 60 of inflammation of the lungs.[8]

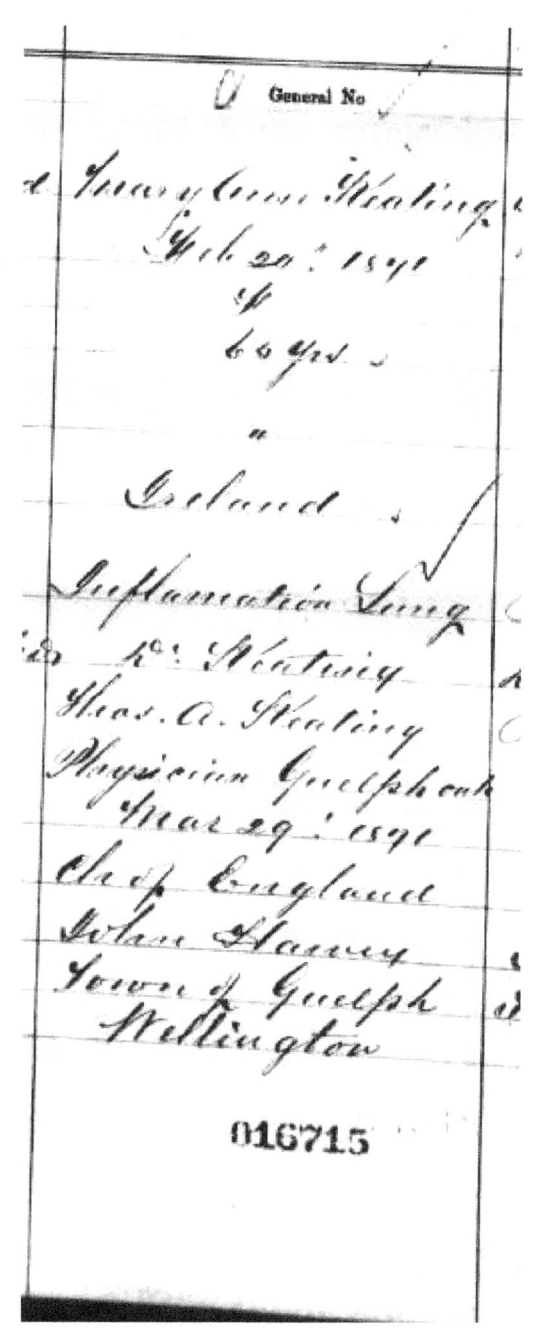

Fig.3. Death Record of Mary A. Keating, 20 February 1871

---

[8] Death Record of Mary Ann Keating, 20 February 1871, Ontario, Canada, Deaths, 1869-1938 & Deaths Overseas, 1939-1947. Ancestry.com. Provo, UT, USA: Ancestry.com Operations, Inc., 2010

She was buried on Wednesday, 22 February 1871 in Woodlawn Cemetery in Guelph.

By 1881 Thomas Keating is residing in a hotel in Guelph, listed as a widower, age 77 and working as a Register of the Surrogate Court.[9]

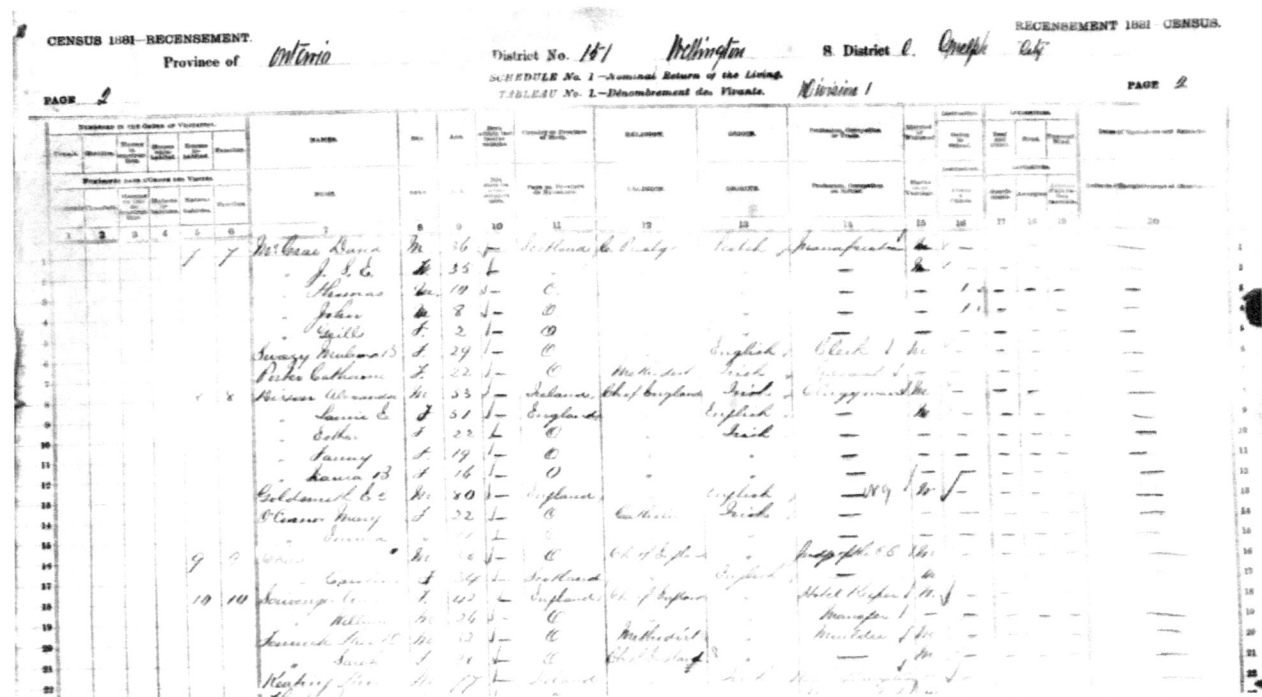

Fig.4. 1881 Canada Census for Guelph, Wellington County, Ontario, Canada listing Thomas Keating (Last entry)

Death of Thomas Keating

Thomas Keating died on Friday, 12 May 1882 of cancer at the age of 78 at Guelph.[10]

---

[9] 1881 Canada Census for Guelph, Wellington County, Ontario, Canada; Page 2, Line 22

[10] Death Record of Thomas Keating, 12 May 1882, Ontario, Canada, Deaths, 1869-1938 & Deaths Overseas, 1939-1947. Ancestry.com. Provo, UT, USA: Ancestry.com Operations, Inc., 2010

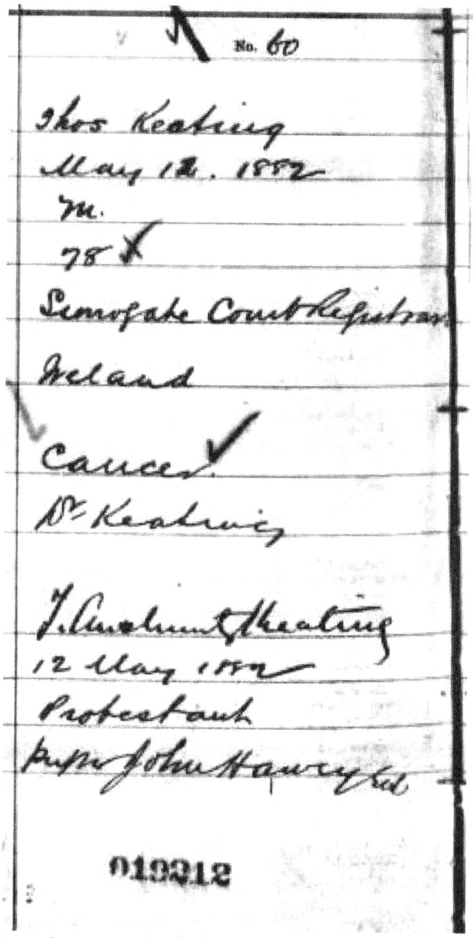

Fig.5. Death Record of Thomas Keating, 12 May 1882

He was buried next to his wife in Woodlawn Cemetery (Block O, Row 12) on Sunday, 14 May 1882 in Guelph. His gravestone reads: "In Memory of Thomas Keating, who departed this life May 12, 1882 aged 78 years. Nothing in my hand I bring. Simply to the cross I cling."

Thomas Keating is warmly commemorated in grateful esteem and recognition by his third great grand-nephew, Michael T. Tracy. This work is dedicated to the Memory of Thomas Keating.

Memoratus in aeternum (Forever Remembered)

Copyright © 2016 Michael T. Tracy

Thomas Auchmuty Keating (1837-1892): A Tribute to his Life and Times
By His Distant Cousin, Michael T. Tracy

Thomas Auchmuty Keating had chosen the medical profession early in his school years and became the first medical doctor of the Keating family. He traveled to London and attended the Royal College of Surgeons being the first Canadian to enroll, a distinction of no ordinary character.[1] Dr. Keating would return to Guelph in 1868 and entered into partnership with Dr. John Howitt and practiced medicine as a physician and surgeon. He would continue the practice long after Dr. Howitt's death in Guelph. Keating was a well-respected doctor for many years until his untimely and tragic death on the morning of Sunday, 13 March 1892 when he overturned his reading lamp. This then is the narrative of the life and times of Thomas Auchmuty Keating.

Early years

Thomas Auchmuty Keating was born on Monday, 30 October 1837 in Guelph.[2] He was the first child of Thomas Keating, Register of the Surrogate Court and Mary Ann Richardson. He attended the Toronto School of Medicine and subsequently traveled to London where he attended the Royal College of Surgeons becoming the first Canadian to enroll in the prestigious school.[3]

Marriage and Family life

Thomas Keating met and later married Elizabeth (Eliza) Orton sometime before 1865-66. They had seven children who were born in Puslinch Township and Guelph. They were:

Thomas Auchmuty born on Sunday, 16 September 1866 and died on Sunday, 23 February 1930;[4]
Constance Georgina born on Thursday, 16 July 1868 and died on Tuesday, 12 March 1935;[5]
John Howitt born on Tuesday, 15 March 1870[6] and died on Tuesday, 23 August 1870;
Mary Ann Richardson born on Wednesday, 15 March 1871;[7]
Richard Orton born on Thursday, 6 June 1872[8] and died on Saturday, 17 July 1886;[9]
Robert Norton born on Friday, 10 September 1875[10] and died on Saturday, 22 August 1903;[11]

---

[1] *Guelph Daily Mercury Newspaper*, 14 March 1892 p. 1

[2] Death Record of Thomas A. Keating, 13 March 1892, Ontario, Canada, Deaths, 1869-1938 & Deaths Overseas, 1939-1947. Ancestry.com. Provo, UT, USA: Ancestry.com Operations, Inc., 2010

[3] *Guelph Daily Mercury Newspaper*, 14 March 1892 p. 1

[4] Death Record of Thomas A. Keating, 23 February 1930, Ontario, Canada, Deaths, 1869-1938 & Deaths Overseas, 1939-1947. Ancestry.com. Provo, UT, USA: Ancestry.com Operations, Inc., 2010

[5] Death Record of Constance G. Lea, 12 March 1935, Ontario, Canada, Deaths, 1869-1938 & Deaths Overseas, 1939-1947. Ancestry.com. Provo, UT, USA: Ancestry.com Operations, Inc., 2010

[6] Birth Record of John Howitt Keating, 15 March 1870, Ontario, Canada, Births, 1869-1913. Ancestry.com. Provo, UT, USA: Ancestry.com Operations, Inc., 2010

[7] Birth Record of Mary Ann Richardson Keating, 15 March 1871, Ontario, Canada, Births, 1869-1913. Ancestry.com. Provo, UT, USA: Ancestry.com Operations, Inc., 2010

[8] Birth Record of Richard Orton Keating, 6 June 1872, Ontario, Canada, Births, 1869-1913. Ancestry.com. Provo, UT, USA: Ancestry.com Operations, Inc., 2010

[9] Death Record of Richard O. Keating, 17 July 1886, Ontario, Canada, Deaths, 1869-1938 & Deaths Overseas, 1939-1947. Ancestry.com. Provo, UT, USA: Ancestry.com Operations, Inc., 2010

[10] Birth Record of Robert Norton Keating, 10 September 1875, Ontario, Canada, Births, 1869-1913. Ancestry.com. Provo, UT, USA: Ancestry.com Operations, Inc., 2010

[11] Death Record of Robert N. Keating, 22 August 1903, Ontario, Canada, Deaths, 1869-1938 & Deaths Overseas, 1939-1947. Ancestry.com. Provo, UT, USA: Ancestry.com Operations, Inc., 2010

Florence Eliza born on Wednesday, 29 August 1877[12] and died on Saturday, 13 February 1965.

Even before his marriage to Eliza Orton, Thomas began his practice in Morriston, Puslinch Township. He came to the Guelph area in 1868 and entered into partnership with Dr. John Howitt and later purchased the property of Dr. Howitt on Essex Street in Guelph.

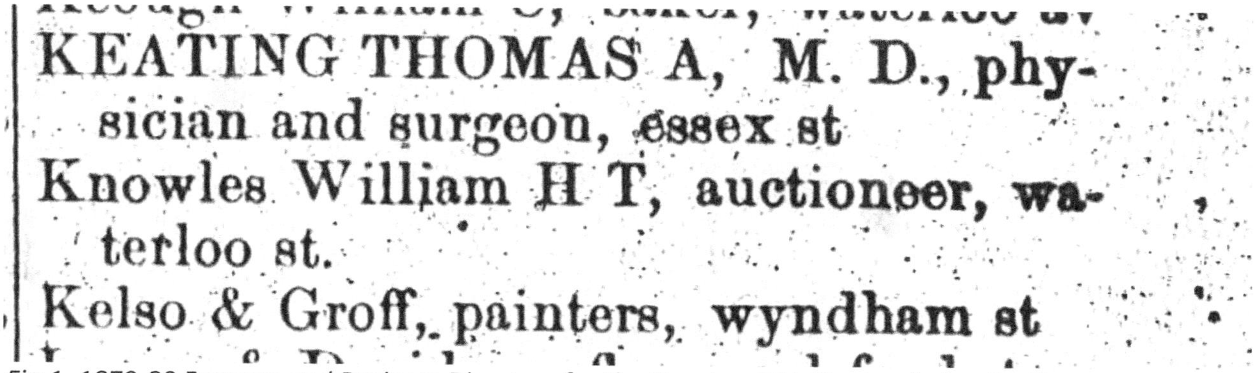

KEATING THOMAS A, M. D., physician and surgeon, essex st
Knowles William H T, auctioneer, waterloo st.
Kelso & Groff, painters, wyndham st

Fig.1. 1879-80 Farmers and Business Directory for the County of Wellington listing Dr. Thomas A. Keating

The Keating family is listed in the 1871 Canada Census for Guelph, Wellington County showing Thomas as being 34 years of age and working as a medical doctor and his wife Eliza is also 34 years of age with the following children: Thomas age 4 and Constance age 2.[13]

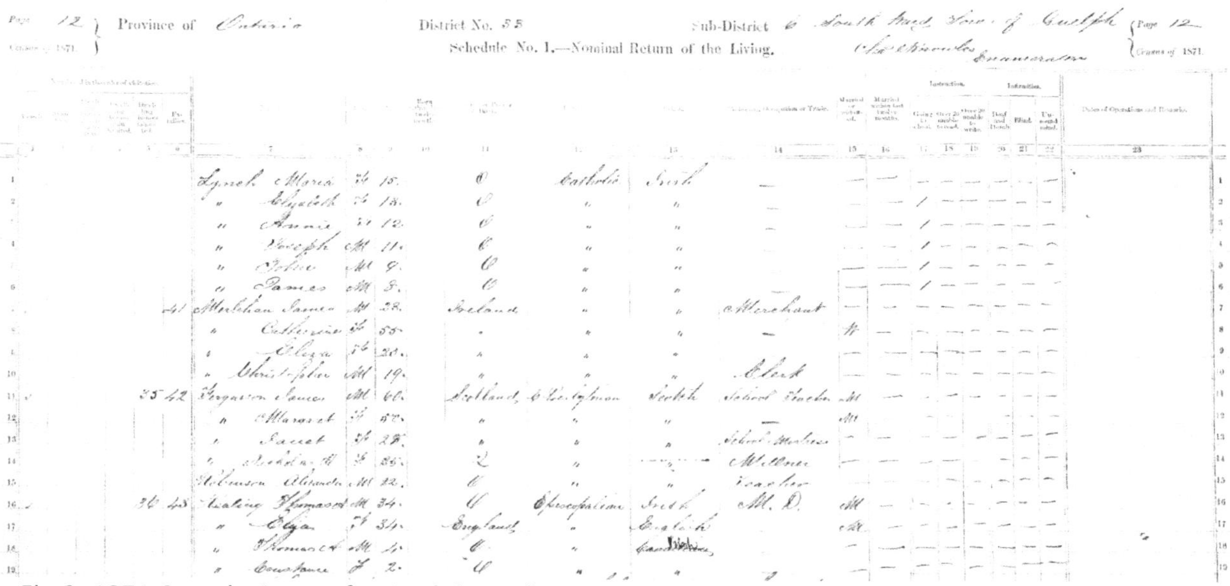

Page 12 Province of Ontario District No. 35 Sub-District South Ward, Town of Guelph Page 12
Census of 1871. Schedule No. 1.—Nominal Return of the Living.

Line			Name	Sex	Age	Born	Religion	Origin	Profession, Occupation or Trade	Married
1			Lynch Maria	F	15.	O	Catholic	Irish	—	
2			" Elizabeth	F	13.	O	"	"	—	
3			" Annie	F	12.	O	"	"	—	
4			" Joseph	M	11.	O	"	"		
5			" John	M	9.	O	"	"		
6			" James	M	8.	O	"	"		
7		41	Moleshan James	M	28.	Ireland	"	"	Merchant	
8			" Catherine	F	55	"	"	"	—	W
9			" Eliza	F	20.	"	"	"		
10			" Christopher	M	19.	"	"	"	Clerk	
11	35	42	Ferguson James	M	60.	Scotland	C. Presbyterian	Scotch	School Teacher	M
12			" Margaret	F	57.	"	"	"	—	M
13			" Janet	F	27.	"	"	"	School Mistress	
14			" Isabella H	F	25.	Q	"		Milliner	
15			Robinson Alexander	M	22.	O	"	"	Teacher	
16	36	43	Keating Thomas	M	34.	O	Episcopalian	Irish	M. D.	M
17			" Eliza	F	34.	England	"	English		M
18			" Thomas A	M	4.	O	"			
19			" Constance	F	2.	O	"	"		

Fig.2. 1871 Canada Census for Guelph, Wellington County, Ontario, Canada listing Thomas A. Keating and Family

---

[12] Birth Record of Florence Eliza Keating, 29 August 1877, Ontario, Canada, Births, 1869-1913. Ancestry.com. Provo, UT, USA: Ancestry.com Operations, Inc., 2010

[13] 1871 Canada Census for Guelph, Wellington County, Ontario, Canada; Page 12, Lines 16-19

Guelph General Hospital

Keating played a large role in the establishment of the Guelph General Hospital.

Fig.3. Guelph General Hospital taken in about 1874, Photograph Courtesy of the Guelph Public Library Archives

"On Monday, 16 August 1875 the hospital opened with 12 beds, a small infectious room and dispensary. The hospital had its own farm on the property that produced and supplied patients with eggs, milk, vegetables and meats."[14] "He was the prime mover in the Guelph General Hospital, and spared no time or pains in having that institution launched on its career of usefulness in the community, and was a constant friend and counsellor of those interested in its success and prosperity."[15] "Citizens will recall with much gratitude his warm cooperation with his sister, Miss Annie Keating, in procuring the ambulance and cab for the sick during the past year."[16]

Member of the Guelph Board of Education

Keating was elected two terms as a member of the Guelph Board of Education during the 1880s and also served two terms as a High School Trustee. "He discharged the duties with signal ability exhibiting much interest in the welfare of the schools and making many admirable suggestions for the improvement of the city education interest."[17] "He bestowed much thought in having the minimum of school children

---

[14] Guelph General Hospital. Accessed at: www.gghorgo.ca
[15] *Guelph Daily Mercury Newspaper*, 14 March 1892 p. 1
[16] *Guelph Daily Mercury Newspaper*, 14 March 1892 p. 1
[17] *Guelph Daily Mercury Newspaper*, 14 March 1892 p. 1

reduced, and prepared a convincing and painstaking circular to be distributed so as to memorialize the Government to have the evil abated of forcing children into our schools at a premature age."[18]

According to the 1881 Canada Census for Guelph, Wellington County Thomas is listed as being 43 years of age and working as a doctor and his wife Eliza is also 43 years of age with the following children: Thomas age 14; Constance age 12; Mary Ann age 10; Richard age 8; Robert age 5; Florence age 3.[19]

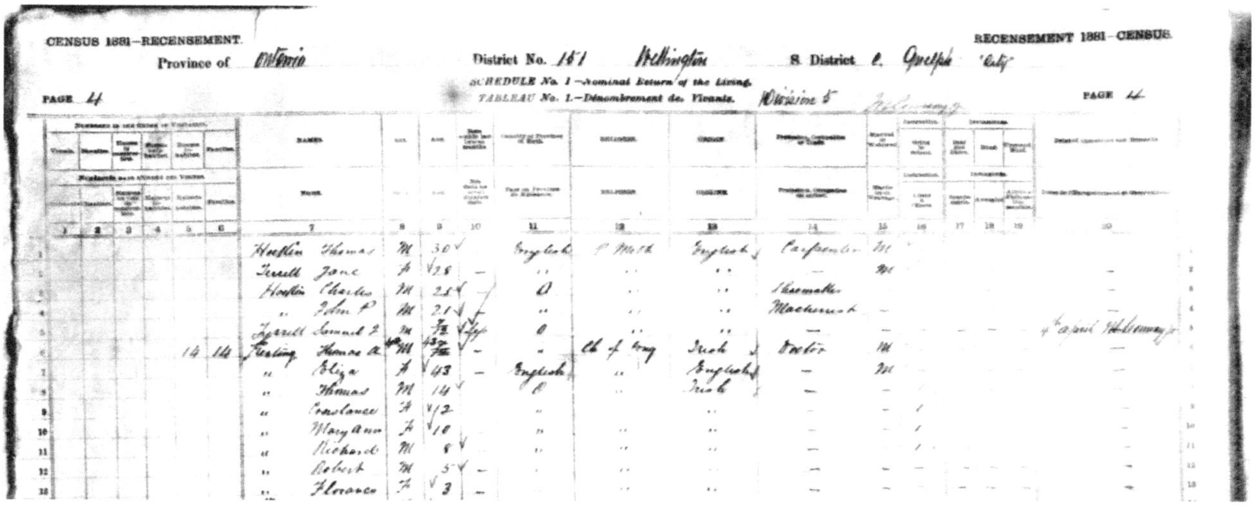
CENSUS 1881—RECENSEMENT. Province of Ontario District No. 161 Wellington S. District e. Guelph 'City' RECENSEMENT 1881—CENSUS.
SCHEDULE No. 1—Nominal Return of the Living. TABLEAU No. 1—Dénombrement des Vivants. Division 5
PAGE 4 PAGE 4

Line	1	2	Names (7)	Sex (8)	Age (9)	Birthplace (11)	Religion (12)	Origin (13)	Profession (14)	Married (15)
1			Hoeklin Thomas	M	30	English	P Meth	English	Carpenter	M
2			Terrell Jane	F	28	"	"	"	—	M
3			Hoeklin Charles	M	25	O	"	"	Shoemaker	
4			" John P	M	21	"	"	"	Machinist	—
5			Terrell Samuel F	M	7/12	O	"	"	—	—
6	14	14	Keating Thomas A	M	43	–	Ch of Eng	Irish	Doctor	M
7			" Eliza	F	43	English	"	English	—	M
8			" Thomas	M	14	O	"	Irish	—	—
9			" Constance	F	12	"		"	—	—
10			" Mary Ann	F	10	"	"	"	—	—
11			" Richard	M	8	"	"	"	—	—
12			" Robert	M	5		"	"	—	—
13			" Florence	F	3		"	"	—	—

Fig.4. 1881 Canada Census for Guelph, Wellington County, Ontario, Canada listing Thomas Keating and Family

The Keating family is listed in the 1891 Canada Census for Guelph, Wellington County listing Thomas as being 54 years of age and working as a physician and his wife Eliza is also 54 years of age with the following children: Constance age 22; Mary age 20; Robert age 15 and working as a hardware clerk; Florence age 13.[20]

<u>Death of Thomas Keating</u>

According to the *Guelph Daily Mercury Newspaper* of Monday, 14 March 1892 is the account of the death of Dr. Thomas A. Keating: "At twenty-five minutes past twelve o'clock Sunday morning the fire alarm was given from the residence of Dr. Keating, Essex Street. The fire brigade was on hand in quick time and a few of the citizens, who witness a sigh which they will not forget to their dying day, as the dead body of Dr. Keating was borne to an adjoining house for fear the fire would spread to the rest of the house. When the citizens generally heard the news on Sunday morning they were more than surprised and could scarcely credit the fact... About a year ago he had a very severe attack of grip, and was laid up for quite a time, and never fully recovered. A month ago he contracted a severe cold by being set fast in a snow drift in the country while visiting a patient, and was prostrated for a few days. Shortly after being able to attend to his practice again he took another slight cold. This he endeavored to shake off although feeling far from well and only a few of his intimate friends knew what he suffered, being troubled with spasms of the heart and an affliction of the lungs. On Saturday he visited his

---

18 *Guelph Daily Mercury Newspaper*, 14 March 1892 p. 1

19 1881 Canada Census for Guelph, Wellington County, Ontario, Canada; Page 4, Lines 6-13

20 1891 Canada Census for Guelph, Wellington County, Ontario, Canada; Pages 64-65, Lines 23-3

patients in the country and town and returned in the evening to his family and spent a few pleasant evening with them. About half past ten or eleven o'clock, he read family prayers and withdrew to his consulting room as was his custom to make up his books, read, write letters, or wait for some call to be made on a patient. About twelve o'clock the servant smelt smoke in her room which is immediately above the consulting room, and awakened Miss Constance Keating. They discovered where the smoke was coming from and telephoned with promptitude to the fire station, after which they aroused the household. Then it was discovered that the doctor was not in his bedroom. The daughter then ran to the consulting room and saw her father sitting in front of his desk with his knees a little bent forward and his hands thrown backward over the chair, while oil was dripping from an upturned lamp in front of him. There were a quantity of papers on the table and it is evident that the doctor had been writing. Mr. C. Grange came to Miss Keating's assistance but was unable to carry the doctor out. Fireman George Hewer arrived a moment or two after and they carried the doctor to the residence of Mr. John R. Redwood, on account of the danger of the fire, as before mentioned, and two physicians sent for, Drs. Howitt and McKinnon. They [were] at the house almost immediately and pronounced that Dr. Keating had been dead for fully an hour as rigor mortis had set in. The grief of the family, on hearing this, was heart-rending, and Mrs. Keating fainted. The doctors thought the cause of death heart failure. Four of them examined the house yesterday, and came to the conclusion that when the spasm seized the doctor, he had fallen forward, thrown out his arms and overturned the lamp, or else that the lamp exploded, thus causing the fire. The report that he died from suffocation is altogether unfounded, as he must have been dead before the fire started. All the damage done by the fire was a burned hole in the carpet and a portion of the wood work scorched near where the lamp had fallen. The brigade soon had the blaze out, but the house was filled with smoke. A post-mortem examination was held this morning by Dr. Howitt, McKinnon and Brock, when it was found that the deceased had suffered from a chronic heart trouble for years, and that his death was due to the rupture of a blood vessel at the base of the heart."[21]

Thomas Auchmuty Keating died on Sunday, 13 March 1892 of heart disease at the age of 54.[22]

---

[21] *Guelph Daily Mercury Newspaper*, 14 March 1892 p. 1

[22] Death Record of Thomas A. Keating, 13 March 1892, Ontario, Canada, Deaths, 1869-1938 & Deaths Overseas, 1939-1947. Ancestry.com. Provo, UT, USA: Ancestry.com Operations, Inc., 2010

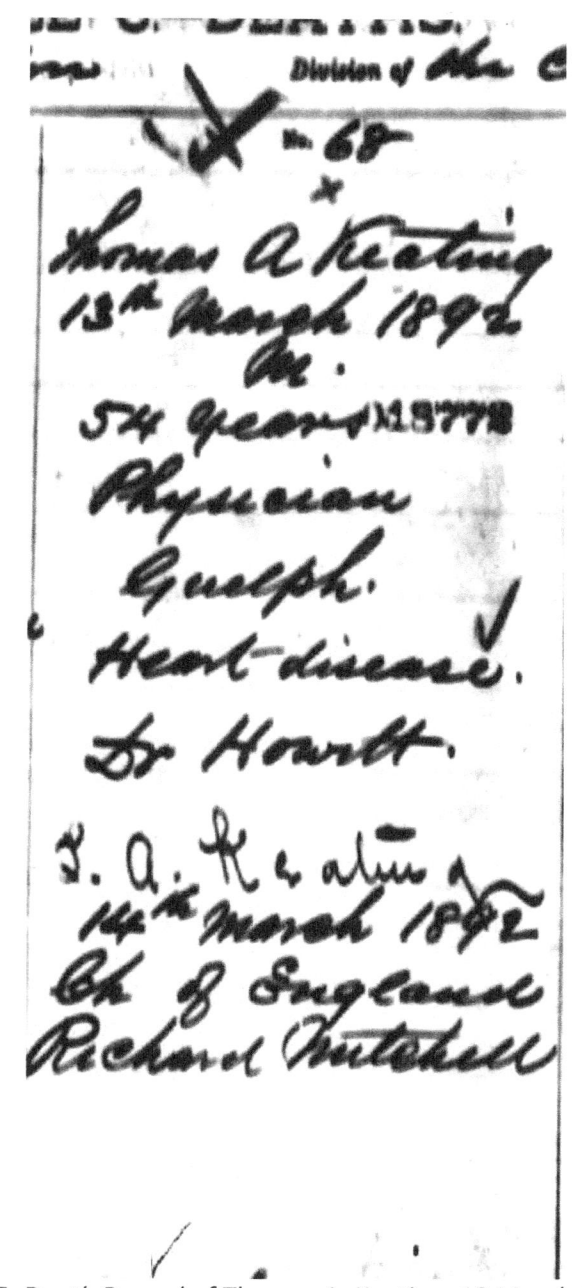

Fig.5. Death Record of Thomas A. Keating, 13 March 1892

He was buried on Tuesday, 15 March 1892 in Woodlawn Cemetery (Block O, Row 12) in Guelph. The *Canadian Practitioner* stated on Friday, 1 April 1892: "Thomas A. Keating, M.D., one of the best known western physicians was Dr. Thomas A. Keating, of Guelph, and the news of his sudden death, March 13, 1892 was heard with deep regret by his many friends. He had for many years a large practice in Guelph and vicinity, and was held in high esteem by his brother practitioners. He became a member of the Royal College of Surgeons in England in 1860, and received his degree of M.D. from Victoria University in 1861."[23]

---

[23] *Canadian Practitioner*, 1 April 1893 p. 168

Death of Eliza Keating

Eliza Keating died on Saturday, 11 March 1899 at the age of 63 of pneumonia and influenza in Guelph.[24]

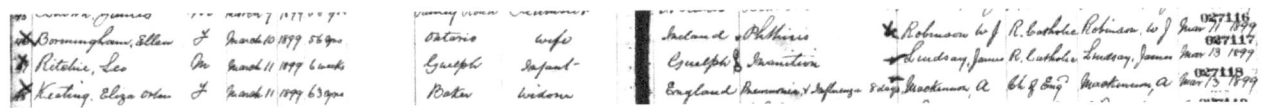

Fig.6. Death Record of Eliza Keating, 11 March 1899

She was buried next to her husband in Woodlawn Cemetery (Block O, Row 12) on Tuesday, 14 March 1899 in Guelph.

Fig.7. Graves of Thomas and Eliza Keating, Woodlawn Cemetery, Guelph, Ontario, Canada, Photograph Courtesy of Michael T. Tracy © 2010 Michael T. Tracy

---

[24] Death Record of Eliza Keating, 11 March 1899, Ontario, Canada, Deaths, 1869-1938 & Deaths Overseas, 1939-1947. Ancestry.com. Provo, UT, USA: Ancestry.com Operations, Inc., 2010

Thomas Auchmuty Keating is warmly commemorated in grateful esteem and recognition by his distant cousin, Michael T. Tracy. This work is dedicated to the Memory of Thomas Auchmuty Keating.

Memoratus in aeternum (Forever Remembered)

Copyright © 2016 Michael T. Tracy

Jemima Mary (Keating) Lamprey (1840-1916): A Tribute to Her Life and Times
By Her Distant Cousin, Michael T. Tracy

Jemima Mary Keating lived in Guelph for all of her life. She was the daughter of Thomas Keating, the Register of the Surrogate Court. Jemima did not marry until much later in life and married the former Mayor of Guelph, John Andrew Lamprey. Jemima Lamprey was a member of the Guelph Social Register for the years 1911-13. This Register was published by the Watchful Circle of the Kings Daughter and Jemima was listed each year in its pages. This then is a narrative of the life and times of Jemima Mary (Keating) Lamprey.

Early years

Jemima Mary Keating was born on Friday, 1 May 1840 in Guelph, Wellington County, Ontario, Canada.[1] She was the second child of Thomas Keating, Register of the Surrogate Court, and Mary Ann Richardson. She is listed in the 1861 Canada Census for Guelph, Wellington County as being 19 years of age.[2]

1861 Canada Census for Guelph, Wellington County, Ontario, Canada listing Jemima Keating

According to the 1871 Canada Census for Guelph Jemima is 26 years of age and residing with her father, Thomas and her sisters Jane and Annie.[3]

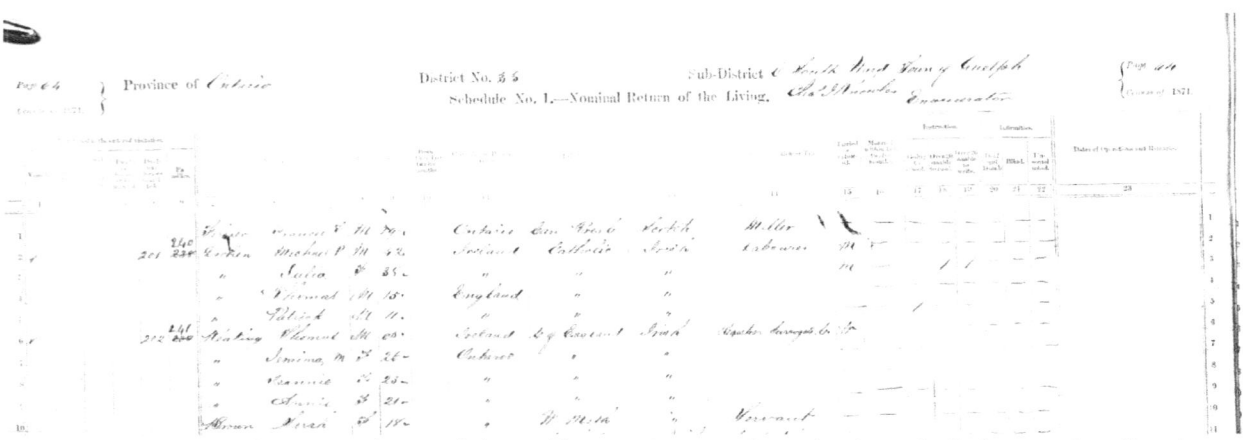

Fig.2. 1871 Canada Census for Guelph, Wellington County, Ontario, Canada listing Jemima Keating

---

[1] Death Record of Jemima M. Lamprey, 30 May 1916, Ontario, Canada, Deaths, 1869-1938 & Deaths Overseas, 1939-1947. Ancestry.com. Provo, UT, USA: Ancestry.com Operations, Inc., 2010
[2] 1861 Canada Census for Guelph, Wellington County, Ontario, Canada; Page 39, Line 44
[3] 1871 Canada Census for Guelph, Wellington County, Ontario, Canada; Page 64, Line 7

Living with her Brother and His Family

By 1881 Jemima Keating and her sisters Jane and Annie resided with her brother Dr. Thomas A. Keating and his family on Essex Street in Guelph. This is evidenced by the 1881 Canada Census for Guelph listing Jemima as being 41 years of age.[4]

Fig.3. 1881 Canada Census for Guelph, Wellington County, Ontario, Canada listing Jemima Keating

According to the 1901 Canada Census for Guelph Jemima is listed as being 60 years of age and residing with her sisters Jane and Anna along with her nieces Mary and Florence.[5]

Fig.4. 1901 Canada Census for Guelph, Wellington County, Ontario, Canada listing Jemima Keating

Marriage to John Andrew Lamprey

John Andrew Lamprey was born at sea in about 1832. He resided on Waterloo Avenue in Guelph since 1879.[6] In 1880 he ran for Alderman and won the election and represented the St. James Ward until 1892. John A. Lamprey ran for Mayor of Guelph and won this election and became Mayor of the City of Guelph in 1895 and served until 1896.

---

[4] 1881 Canada Census for Guelph, Wellington County, Ontario, Canada; Page 4, Line 14
[5] 1901 Canada Census for Guelph, Wellington County, Ontario, Canada; Page 9, Lines 44-48
[6] *Guelph Daily Mercury Newspaper*, 4 September 1879 p. 1

Fig.5. Mayor John A. Lamprey taken in 1895, Photograph Courtesy of the Guelph Public Library Archives

Fig.6. Mayor John A. Lamprey (Second from right) on Heffernan Bridge with St. George's Church in background taken in 1896, Photograph Courtesy of the Guelph Public Library Archives

Jemima Keating met and later married the former Mayor of Guelph on Wednesday, 3 August 1904.[7]

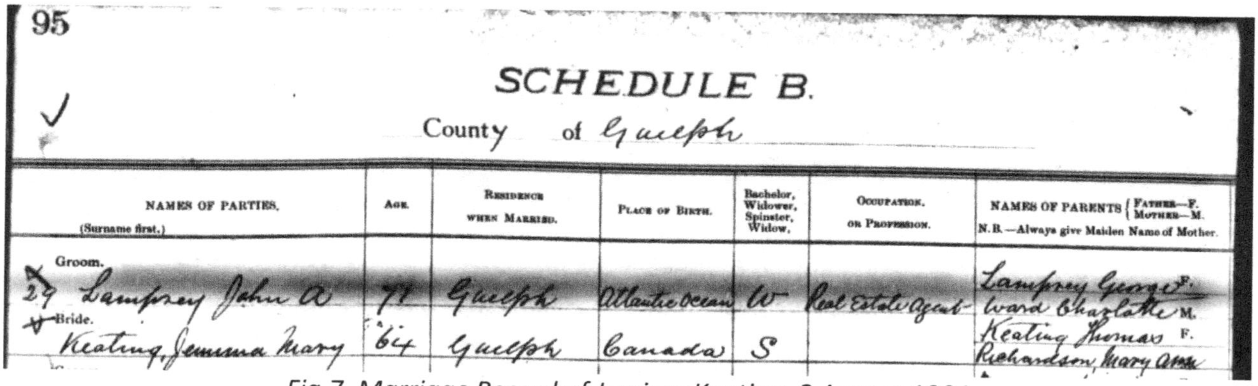

95

SCHEDULE B.

County of Guelph

NAMES OF PARTIES. (Surname first.)	AGE.	RESIDENCE WHEN MARRIED.	PLACE OF BIRTH.	Bachelor, Widower, Spinster, Widow.	OCCUPATION, OR PROFESSION.	NAMES OF PARENTS {FATHER—F. MOTHER—M. N.B.—Always give Maiden Name of Mother.
Groom. 29 Lamprey John A	71	Guelph	Atlantic Ocean	W	Real Estate Agent	Lamprey George F. Ward Charlotte M.
Bride. Keating, Jemima Mary	64	Guelph	Canada	S		Keating Thomas F. Richardson, Mary Ann

Fig.7. Marriage Record of Jemima Keating, 3 August 1904

According to the *Historical Atlas of the County of Wellington*: "In church work [John A. Lamprey] is equally enviable, as he was for twelve years Chairman of the Board of Managers of St. Andrews Presbyterian Church, and two years member of the Board of Managers of Knox Church, which he still attends. After six years of experience Mr. Lamprey, in 1887, opened his present office, where, since that date, he has conducted a loan, real estate, insurance and conveyancing business."[8]

Death of John A. Lamprey

John A. Lamprey died on Saturday, 24 May 1913 of pneumonia at the age of 81.[9]

---

[7] Marriage Record of Jemima Keating, 3 August 1904, Ontario, Canada, Marriages, 1801-1928. Ancestry.com & Genealogical Research Library. Provo, UT, USA: Ancestry.com Operations, Inc., 2010

[8] *Historical Atlas of the County of Wellington, Ontario, Canada*. Toronto: Historical Atlas Publishing Co., 1906

[9] Death Record of John A. Lamprey, 24 May 1913, Ontario, Canada, Deaths, 1869-1938 & Deaths Overseas, 1939-1947. Ancestry.com. Provo, UT, USA: Ancestry.com Operations, Inc., 2010

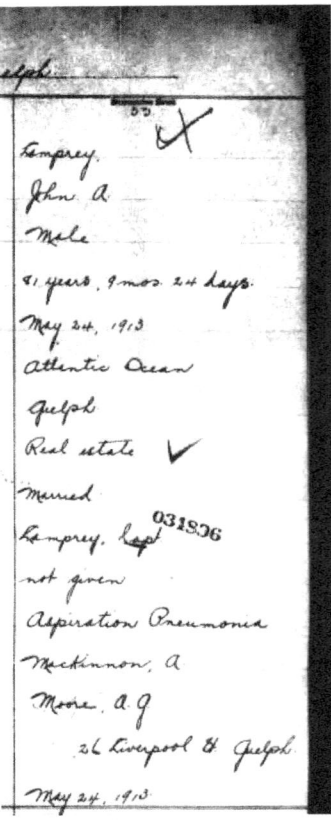

Fig.8. Death Record of John A. Lamprey, 24 May 1913

He was buried on Monday, 26 May 1913 in Woodlawn Cemetery (Block 0, Row 17) next to his first wife and children.

Fig.9. Grave of John A. Lamprey and Family, Woodlawn Cemetery, Guelph, Ontario, Canada, Photograph Courtesy of Michael T. Tracy © 2010 Michael T. Tracy

Death of Jemima Lamprey

Jemima Mary Lamprey died on Tuesday, 30 May 1916 of pneumonia at the age of 76 in Guelph.[10]

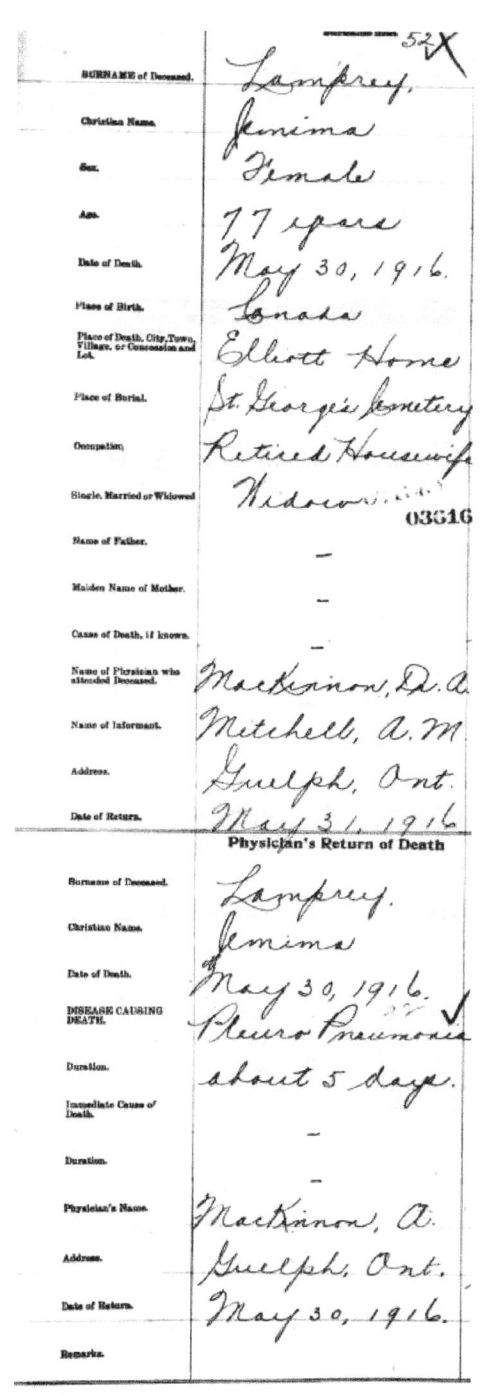

Fig.10. Death Record of Jemima Lamprey, 30 May 1916

---

[10] Death Record of Jemima M. Lamprey, 30 May 1916, Ontario, Canada, Deaths, 1869-1938 & Deaths Overseas, 1939-1947. Ancestry.com. Provo, UT, USA: Ancestry.com Operations, Inc., 2010

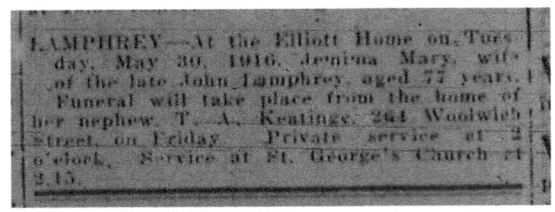

Fig.11. Obituary Notice of Jemima Lamprey, Guelph Mercury Newspaper, 30 May 1916

She was buried in Woodlawn Cemetery (Block 0, Row 11) on Wednesday, 31 May 1916.

Fig.12. Grave of Jemima Lamprey, Woodlawn Cemetery, Guelph, Ontario, Canada, Photograph Courtesy of Michael T. Tracy © 2010 Michael T. Tracy

Jemima (Keating) Lamprey is warmly commemorated in grateful esteem and recognition by her distant cousin, Michael T. Tracy. This work is dedicated to the Memory of Jemima (Keating) Lamprey.

Memoratus in aeternum (Forever Remembered)

Copyright © 2016 Michael T. Tracy

Jane Keating (1846-1928): A Tribute to Her Life and Times
By Her Distant Cousin, Michael T. Tracy

Jane Keating was the third child of Thomas Keating, the Register of the Surrogate Court, and spent her entire life in Guelph. She was a spinster and lived a quiet life. This then is the narrative of the life and times of Jane Keating.

Early years

Jane Keating was born on Tuesday, 17 February 1846 in Guelph, Wellington County, Ontario, Canada.[1] She was the third child of Thomas Keating, Register of the Surrogate Court, and Mary Ann Richardson. She was listed in the 1861 Canada Census for Guelph as being 16 years of age.[2]

Fig.1. 1861 Canada Census for Guelph, Wellington County, Ontario, Canada listing Jane Keating

By 1871 Jane is residing in Guelph with her father and sisters.[3]

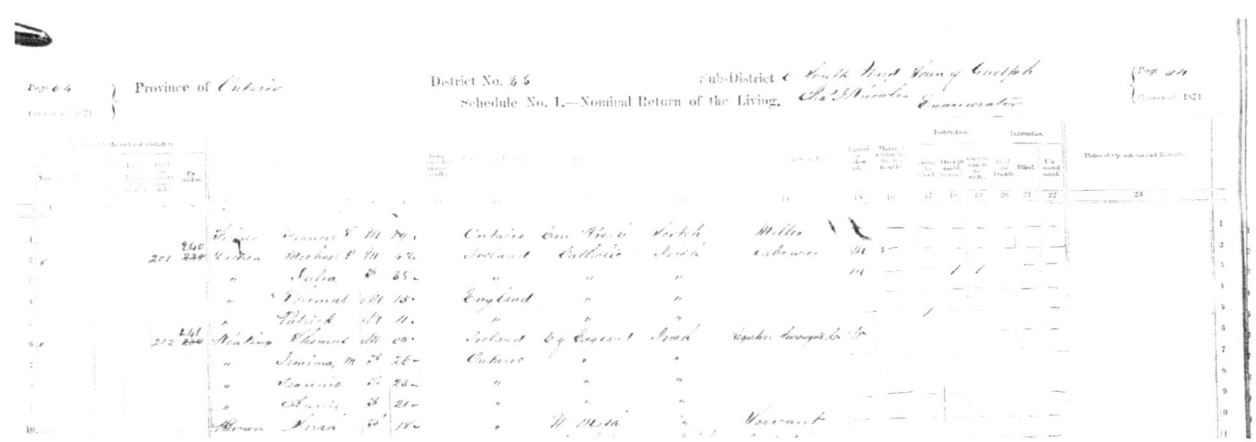

Fig.2. 1871 Canada Census for Guelph, Wellington County, Ontario, Canada listing Jane Keating

Living with her Brother and His Family

According to the 1881 Canada Census for Guelph, Jane is residing with her brother, Dr. Thomas A. Keating and his family on Essex Street and listed as being 36 years of age.[4]

---

[1] Death Record of Jane Keating, 31 December 1928, Ontario, Canada, Deaths, 1869-1938 & Deaths Overseas, 1939-1947. Ancestry.com. Provo, UT, USA: Ancestry.com Operations, Inc., 2010

[2] 1861 Canada Census for Guelph, Wellington County, Ontario, Canada; Page 39, Line 46

[3] 1871 Canada Census for Guelph, Wellington County, Ontario, Canada; Page 64, Line 8

[4] 1881 Canada Census for Guelph, Wellington County, Ontario, Canada; Page 4, Line 15

Fig.3. 1881 Canada Census for Guelph, Wellington County, Ontario, Canada listing Jane Keating

By 1891 she is residing with her sister Anna and nieces and nephews in Guelph.[5]

Fig.4. 1891 Canada Census for Guelph, Wellington County, Ontario, Canada listing Jane Keating

According to the 1901 Canada Census for Guelph she is residing with her sisters Jemima and Anna and her nieces Mary and Florence.[6]

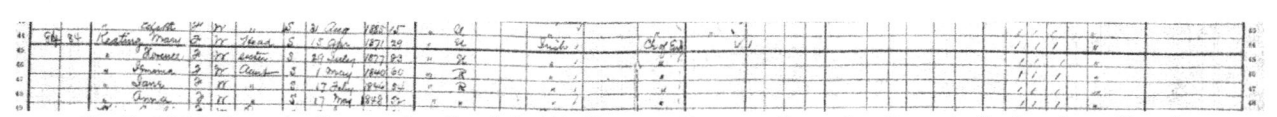

Fig.5. 1901 Canada Census for Guelph, Wellington County, Ontario, Canada listing Jane Keating

---

[5] 1891 Canada Census for Guelph, Wellington County, Ontario, Canada; Page 65, Line 4

[6] 1901 Canada Census for Guelph, Wellington County, Ontario, Canada; Page 9, Line 47

Death of Jane Keating

Jane Keating died on Monday, 31 December 1928 of congestion of the lungs at the age of 82 at the Elliot Home in Guelph which was near the Guelph General Hospital.[7]

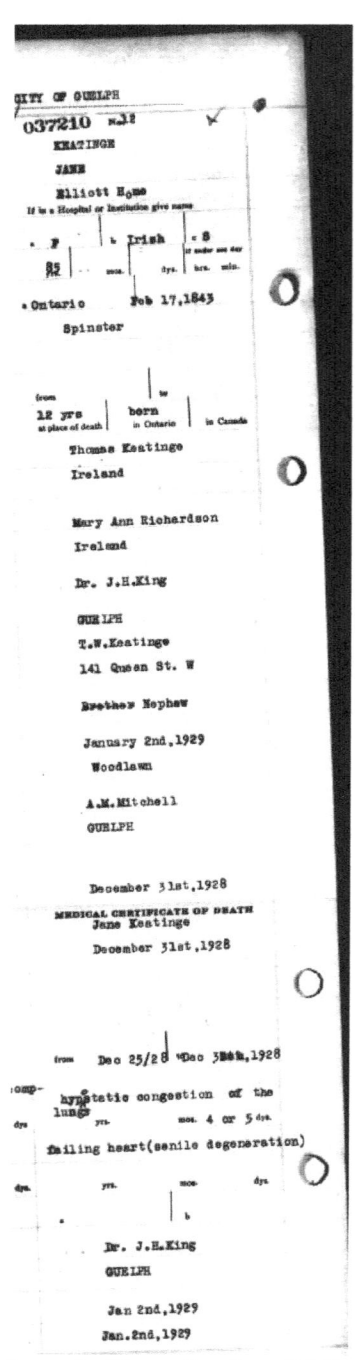

Fig.6. Death Record of Jane Keating, 31 December 1928

---

[7] Death Record of Jane Keating, 31 December 1928, Ontario, Canada, Deaths, 1869-1938 & Deaths Overseas, 1939-1947. Ancestry.com. Provo, UT, USA: Ancestry.com Operations, Inc., 2010

Jane Keating was buried in Woodlawn Cemetery (Block 0, Row 11) on Wednesday, 2 January 1929 in Guelph.

Fig.7. Grave of Jane Keating, Woodlawn Cemetery, Guelph, Ontario, Canada, Photograph Courtesy of Michael T. Tracy © 2010 Michael T. Tracy

Jane Keating is warmly commemorated in grateful esteem and recognition by her distant cousin, Michael T. Tracy. This work is dedicated to the Memory of Jane Keating.

Memoratus in aeternum (Forever Remembered)

Copyright © 2016 Michael T. Tracy

Anna Maria Keating (1848-1930): A Tribute to Her Life and Times
By Her Distant Cousin, Michael T. Tracy

Anna Maria Keating was the fourth child of Thomas Keating, the Register of the Surrogate Court, and spent her entire life in the City of Guelph with her sisters. She was instrumental along with her brother, Dr. Thomas A. Keating, in procuring an ambulance and cab for the sick in 1891.[1] Anna Keating was a spinster and like her sisters lived a quiet life. She would spend her later years in the Elliot Home on the grounds of the Guelph General Hospital. This then is the narrative of the life and times of Anna Maria Keating.

Early years

Anna Maria Keating was born on Wednesday, 17 May 1848 in Guelph, Wellington County, Ontario, Canada.[2] She was the fourth child of Thomas Keating, Register of the Surrogate Court, and Mary Ann Richardson. She was listed in the 1861 Canada Census for Guelph as being 14 years of age.[3]

Fig.1. 1861 Canada Census for Guelph, Wellington County, Ontario, Canada listing Anna Keating

In 1871 Anna is shown as residing with her father and sisters.[4]

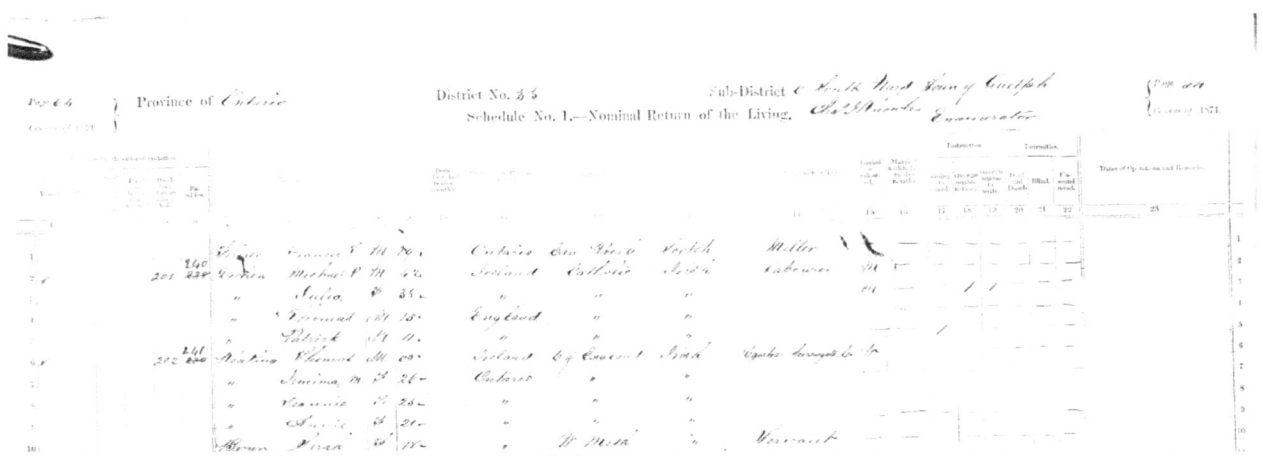

Fig.2. 1871 Canada Census for Guelph, Wellington County, Ontario, Canada listing Anna Keating

---

[1] *Guelph Daily Mercury Newspaper*, 14 March 1892 p. 1

[2] Death Record of Anna Maria Keating, 29 April 1930, Ontario, Canada, Deaths, 1869-1938 & Deaths Overseas, 1939-1947. Ancestry.com. Provo, UT, USA: Ancestry.com Operations, Inc., 2010

[3] 1861 Canada Census for Guelph, Wellington County, Ontario, Canada; Page 39, Line 47

[4] 1871 Canada Census for Guelph, Wellington County, Ontario, Canada; Page 64, Line 9

Living with her Brother and His Family

According to the 1881 Canada Census for Guelph, Anna is residing with her brother Dr. Thomas A. Keating and his family on Essex Street and is listed as being 34 years of age.[5]

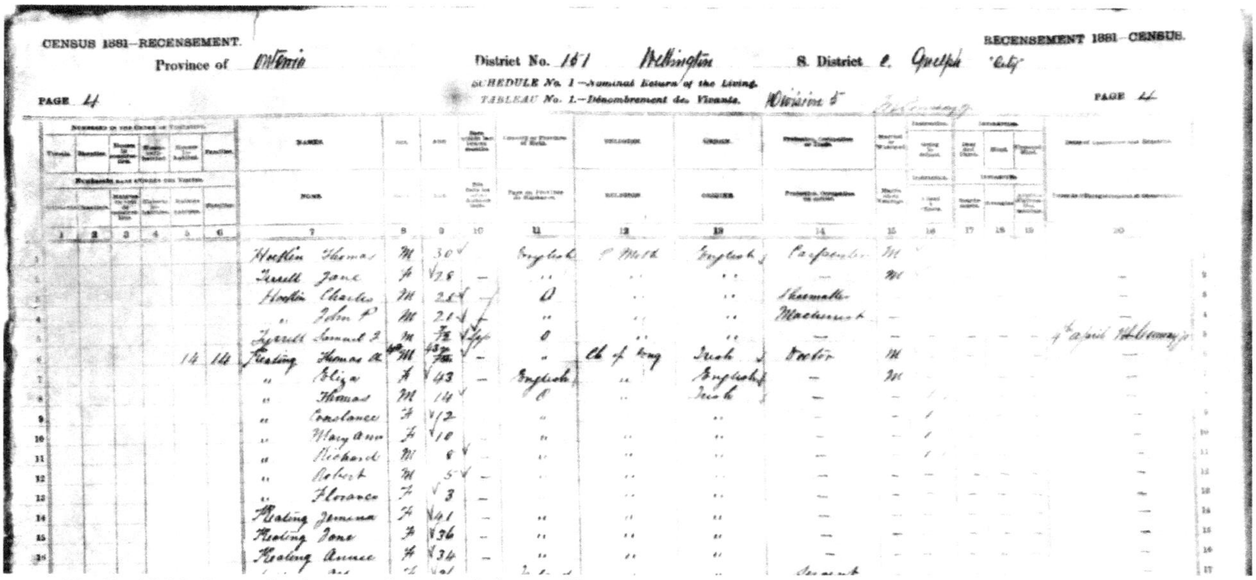

Fig.3. 1881 Canada Census for Guelph, Wellington County, Ontario, Canada listing Anna Keating

By 1891 she is residing with her sister Jane and nieces and nephews in Guelph and is 43 years of age.[6]

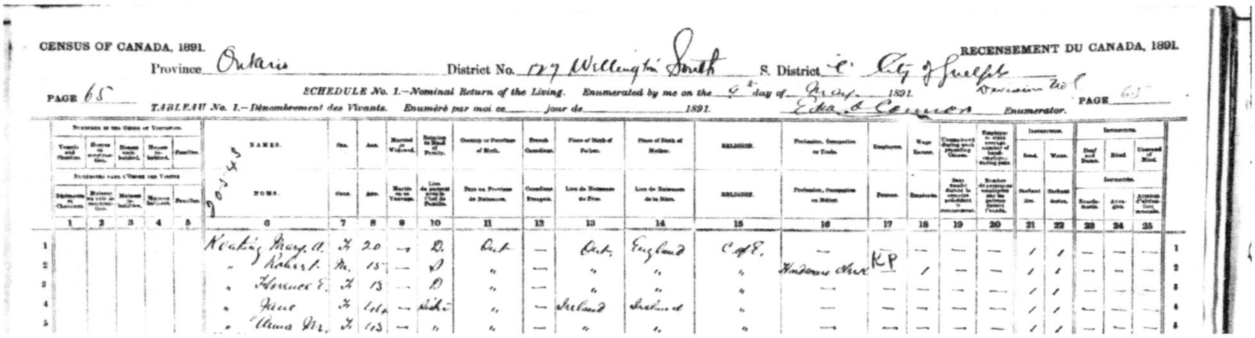

Fig.4. 1891 Canada Census for Guelph, Wellington County, Ontario, Canada listing Anna Keating

Also in 1891 Anna was instrumental along with her brother, Dr. Thomas A. Keating in procuring an ambulance and cab for the sick.[7]

---

[5] 1881 Canada Census for Guelph, Wellington County, Ontario, Canada; Page 4, Line 16
[6] 1891 Canada Census for Guelph, Wellington County, Ontario, Canada; Page 65, Line 5
[7] *Guelph Daily Mercury Newspaper*, 14 March 1892 p. 1

According to the 1901 Canada Census for Guelph Anna is residing with her sisters Jemima and Jane and her nieces and is listed as being 52 years of age.[8]

Fig.5. 1901 Canada Census for Guelph, Wellington County, Ontario, Canada listing Anna Keating

Death of Anna Maria Keating

Anna Maria Keating died on Tuesday, 29 April 1930 of senility at the Elliott Home in Guelph at the age of 81.[9]

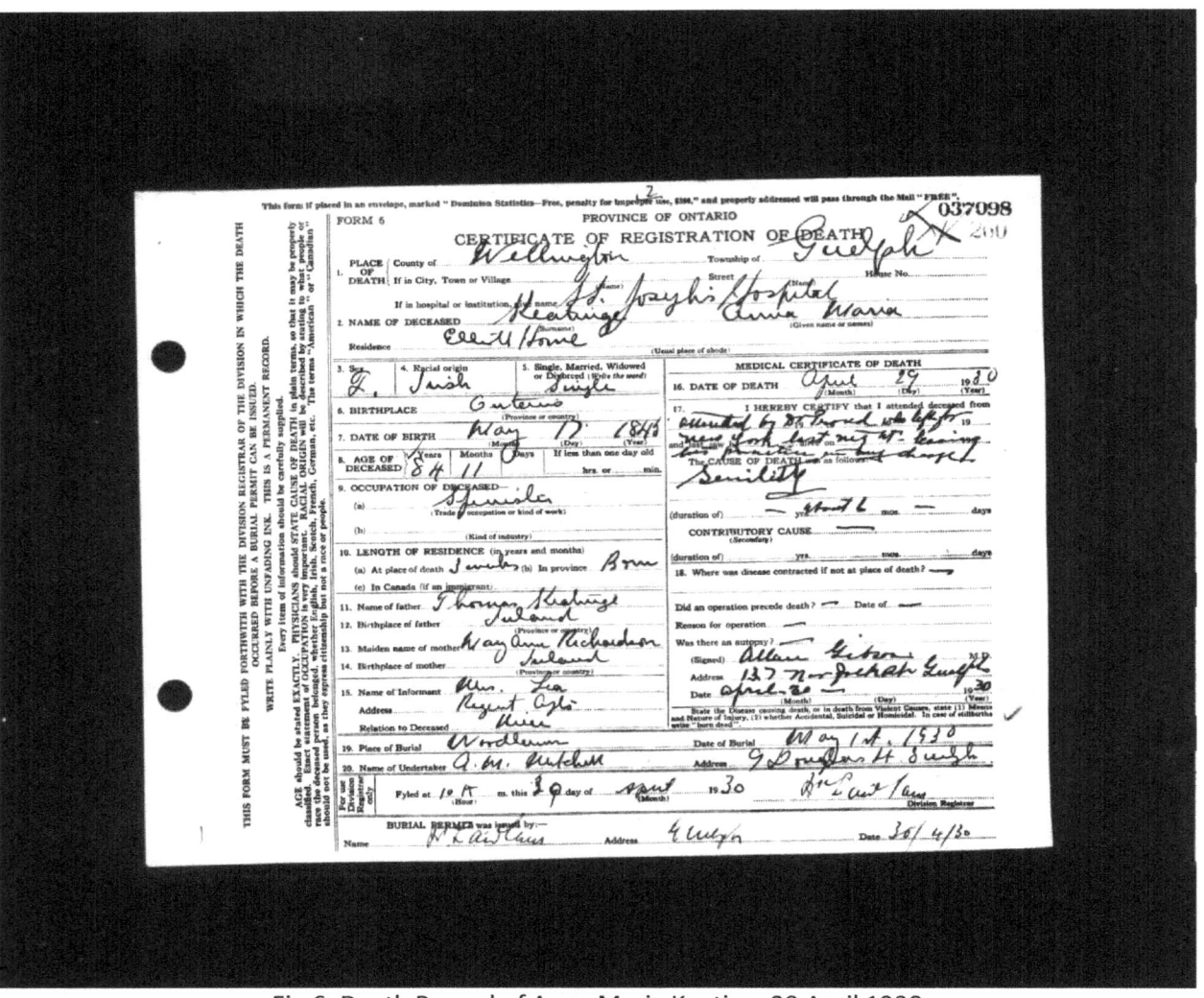

Fig.6. Death Record of Anna Maria Keating, 29 April 1930

---

[8] 1901 Canada Census for Guelph, Wellington County, Ontario, Canada; Page 9, Line 48
[9] Death Record of Anna Maria Keating, 29 April 1930, Ontario, Canada, Deaths, 1869-1938 & Deaths Overseas, 1939-1947. Ancestry.com. Provo, UT, USA: Ancestry.com Operations, Inc., 2010

DEATHS

KEATINGE—Died on April 29th, 1930, Anna Maria Keatinge, youngest and last surviving daughter of the late Thomas Keatinge, Esq.

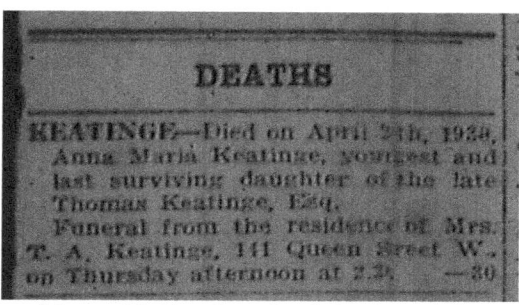

Funeral from the residence of Mrs. T. A. Keatinge, 141 Queen Street W., on Thursday afternoon at 2.30. —30

Fig.7. Obituary Notice of Anna M. Keating, Guelph Mercury Newspaper, 30 April 1930

She was buried next to her sisters in Woodlawn Cemetery (Block 0, Row 11) on Thursday, 1 May 1930.

Fig.8. Grave of Anna M. Keating, Woodlawn Cemetery, Guelph, Ontario, Canada, Photograph Courtesy of Michael T. Tracy © 2010 Michael T. Tracy

Anna Maria Keating is warmly commemorated in grateful esteem and recognition by her distant cousin, Michael T. Tracy. This work is dedicated to the Memory of Anna Maria Keating.

Memoratus in aeternum (Forever Remembered)

Copyright © 2016 Michael T. Tracy

Made in the USA
Middletown, DE
24 December 2018